DANCE LIKE NOBODY'S WATCHING

My Story

By Alis Cerrahyan

Copyright: Alis Cerrahyan, 2016
CAUTION: This is a work of non-fiction. All names, dates and places have been approved by all persons named in the work. All rights reserved. . Except for brief quotations in critical reviews, this work may not be reproduced by any means. The Work is fully protected under the copyright laws of the United States of America, and of all countries covered by the International Copyright Union (including the Dominion of Canada and the rest of the British Commonwealth), and of all countries covered by the Pan-American Copyright Convention, the Universal Copyright Convention, and the Berne Convention, and of all countries with which the United States has reciprocal copyright relations. All rights, including public reading, radio broadcasting, television, video or sound recording, all other forms of mechanical or electronic reproduction, such as CD- ROM, CD-I, DVD, information storage and retrieval systems and photo-copying, and the rights of translation into foreign languages, are strictly reserved.

Published by WordsonPage, an imprint of WordsonStage.net Virginia Beach, Virginia 2016

Cover Painting by Alis Cerrahyan

INTRODUCTION............................4

CHAPTER 1:   Istanbul.............14

CHAPTER 2:   Disaster.............39

CHAPTER 3:   Jirayr..................61

CHAPTER 4:   God....................82

CHAPTER 5:   America.............96

CHAPTER 6:   Blessings...........110

CHAPTER 7:   Business............131

CHAPTER 8:   Forgiveness......146

CHAPTER 9:   Conclusion........162

ACKNOWLEDGMENTS.................177

Copyright: Alis Cerrahyan 2016

Published by WordsonPage, an imprint of WordsonStage.net, Virginia Beach, Virginia, 2016

INTRODUCTION.   WE ARE BROKEN

Life begins when a new person enters into light.   As a baby needs all the love and nurturing he or she can possibly receive to become a grown man or woman, that life goes through stages of maturity and knowledge.   Whether we are born with a silver spoon in our mouth or within the depths of extreme poverty, we all are broken in some way, shape, or form; until we mature enough to recognize it, address it, and step away from it.   Often we spend much time and effort trying to appear perfect, while we know that it's a misguided effort to blend in, and become part of a society that will, sooner or later, incriminate us at any opportunity.   Our goal is always perfection; but we fail to recognize that we already *are* a product of perfection.   Britt Reints, author and speaker on Happiness, helps people reach their maximum potential.   She says it this way; "I can be a work in progress and a perfect work of art all at the same time."

Our brokenness becomes real to us as we walk away from a debilitating situation.   It strikes in many ways at once.   We are fortunate if we recognize it right away.   But most of the time, it lies undetected; because it's woven into our psyche, while we were being shaped and molded into conscious beings.   What is more debilitating about it is that, the longer it takes for us to understand and admit our own weakness, the greater the possibility that we will attract similar situations, because they feel familiar.   I can easily identify situations that disgrace and defame me with the wet mud I wade through once I step in, and from which I never emerge without getting mucked up. Unless we're gods or super-humans, most of us step into life's muddy circumstances, at least once.   What seems horrendous may be a blessing in disguise; an opportunity for us to recognize the bleeding ulcer we carry within.   Without our effort to treat this, it keeps causing us to make the same mistake, over and over again.   We count ourselves extremely lucky if we step away from it, and keep walking until the mud dries out, so we can dust ourselves off.   In fact, the stains left behind become a reminder of what that mud looked and smelled like; so we'll know to avoid it next time around; that is, if there is a next time.

       What happens when we don't admit our weaknesses during the challenges of life?   The answer is simple: we remain in the mud; not knowing that we are free to walk away.   In some cases, we're afraid to step out because we're afraid of the unknown.   We recognize the mud because it's part of who we are as we grew up.   It may be our humiliation by a parent or relative, a teacher or a status symbol, like our possessions... you name it.   We plant ourselves deeply in the mud, smearing it all over ourselves, and even try not miss a spot.   We spend time blaming others for our misfortunes; simply because we're not willing to confess our inadequacy to detect our own flawed nature.   Therefore, we stay put in one spot, as aggressive as one can be, missing out on the rest of life's experiences.

       It is impossible these days to avoid the homeless in our country.   We know they are growing in number.   We see them on street corners during the rush hour.   Some of them may have gotten a bad start from extreme childhood circumstances; or they may have simply blown their lives away by making poor choices; but that isn't the case for every one of them.   Most of those people, at some moment in time, stepped into the mud and stood planted in their circumstances.   They lost sight of their dreams and hopes.   I personally choose to help out by giving them something; even though I know what I give will not help their situation.   It is a simple token of gratitude, proclaiming that I too could have been in their shoes, had it not been for the grace and the mercy of God, which continues to pour upon me the determination to overcome my circumstances.

    I know I cannot generate a super-human version of who I am. I need plenty of help; and I choose calling my help God.   Others may call it "the Universe" or the inner self.   Just as there are many levels of growth in a baby's journey to adulthood, there are many destinies, depending on which we will call our eternal home.   I feel sad for those who have the wind knocked out of their sails, and choose to place themselves at others' mercy for help and provisions; not recognizing the fact that they can start by taking baby steps, and walk away from their unfortunate place.   And I also feel sorry for those who believe they are strong enough to overcome all difficulties, all on their own, like mini-gods; while they crumble into heaps of rubble on the inside.   They address their torments by trying to prove themselves in ways that matter to no one but themselves.   In fact, the harder they try, the less they are satisfied.   Even though they appear strong enough to battle their miseries, they are spiritual and psychological misfits.   You see, it takes growth for someone to admit that he ought to reflect back, observe his progress, and identify his mistakes; rather than attacking the distance he has yet to go, without wiping off some mud occasionally.   It truly takes more courage to walk the distance within the boundaries of his inner self.   And that's a highly important one than the distance he or she aims to go on the outside.

    I wouldn't write this if I didn't have a story to tell.   It may come as a shock to some; but my story is about a certain mud... or two... that I found myself flopping through, on more than one occasion. Let me take time to describe myself. I'm a peace-lover and a peace-seeker. I am no athlete. In fact, I've spent more time sitting on the bleachers as a kid, overcoming injuries, rather than playing the game on the field. Most people who know me today might think I am a competitive athlete wannabe, looking to crush obstacles in a mud run event. I lived through situations that gave me a certain level of experience; but unfortunately, every event is different. For some, there is not enough preparation or   study time, regardless of how full our mental library of reference might be. That's why I am resigned to the fact that I am in need of an external source to provide me with enough determination to make it through life. Otherwise I might dangle at the end of my rope, not knowing when I will have to unclench my fist, and let go of all of my expectations for good. I have survived being let down by many; but I don't know if I can survive the pain of letting myself down. For me, that is a greater loss than what I am willing to allow myself. Such a loss would soil my judgment and reduce my confidence as a decision maker. I have seen many forms of physical handicap in this life; but there is nothing like a spiritual handicap that keeps people paralyzed with one unfortunate experience.

    I am fifty-eight years old, a single mother of two, a business owner for twenty-five years, and a huge believer in Divine provisions. Not a day goes by that I am not reminded of how delicate life is. I'm one breath away, like everybody else out there, from a life changing event. The familiar could fade into a distant memory instantly, giving place to an unfamiliar new stage upon which I may play the lead role. Often, I ask myself, "How did I get here?" "What was I thinking?" or

"Can I have a do-over?"   The questions are endless, but there is only one answer; and it lies within: "You're going to dig yourself out of this one, somehow, and you better make it quick.   Otherwise it's huge enough to become your new residence!"

      I don't like changes; especially those that inflict pain and humiliation.   And part of the reason I decided to write this book is to give these experiences a noble cause; hoping that a reader or two will find my struggles parallel their circumstances.   The greatest victory of my life happened the day I finally recognized my limitations, and stopped pretending to be someone who walked through life, straight as an arrow, while trying to sweep her flaws into a dark corner, where they remained out of sight.   I always knew they were there.   I just didn't want others to see them.   Because their opinion of me was important during those days.   It was shaping me into someone politically correct and socially acceptable; so I wouldn't feel like an outsider.

      I wanted to be like everybody else.   I didn't realize that being different and unique was a gift from above.   I was playing a part, rather than being myself.   Therefore, all of the God-given resources were unnoticed, untouched, and unused.   It was an existence of pretense; but there was no life in it.   With all the resources I possess today; and knowing that God is life and God is love, how did I ever believe that a pretend life could lead to true love?   I remained a disaster ready to happen, with every choice I made, simply because I was afraid to recognize and admit my own flaws.   By putting this in writing, I'm bringing them out of that dark corner, and scattering them; so everyone can get a good look at who I truly am.   To a certain extent, I'm embarrassed to have so many flaws.   But I'm also equally as proud of exposing them to light, where healing can begin.

      I don't want anyone to think I'm dark and depressed.   I'm far from that.   I have experienced moments of occasional depression; but I've been able to see the lighter side of things.   Both my brother and I inherited that quality from our dad, who was a gentle soul.   He wouldn't hurt anyone.   He worked hard all his life to provide for his family.   He stood for what was right, refusing to take shortcuts.   He was determined to smile through it all; and contagiously enough, he brought a smile to others' faces.   He found a refuge - which we discovered after his passing – in his lengthy writings where he created a persona as a radio host.   In those pages we discovered that he was a true comedian.   He had a pretend audience; and there were pages and pages of humor that he never performed.   What we actually failed to recognize is more like the froth of a boiling soup; kind of feathery and white, that we try to skim; thinking it could affect the taste.   But, we overlook the fact that it contains protein necessary for our health.   Dad was full of fun and laughter, which are all the necessary ingredients to heal the soul, as an antidote to decay and other debilitating circumstances.   Laughter was dad's weapon of choice to tear down walls of irritants that made life less enjoyable than it was meant to be.

      Dad loved our mother very much, perhaps with the kind of love she never thought was possible.   Tall, dark and handsome, he exhibited a meek and quiet personality.   He worked hard and supported our family of four beautifully; leaving us with delightful memories that my brother and I will never bury, even years after his passing.   He led an honorable life.   He was a worthy man; a place of patience, peace and happiness; a common denominator, mediating chaos of all kinds. He exuded love. He had plenty of it for everyone; and he definitely overindulged us.

What have I learned from Dad? I've learned that the best legacy I can leave behind is a collage of un-preached sermons demonstrated by practical deeds; restraint from unnecessary negativity; and meaningful ways to make a difference in others' lives. I'd like to live so that when my two children think of words like contentment, integrity, kindness, and fairness, they'll think of me. I'd like them to follow my example, only because it would mean a lot to them. Not that I want them to forget how many times I've hit the ground. But I certainly want them to always remember how well I rose after each fall.

There were times I didn't think I would be able to raise two kids by myself; not because they were being difficult; but because I didn't have enough confidence to do the job right. Growing up as a straight-A student and an overachiever gave me a false confidence, until I found myself divorced with two kids. I didn't know what to do with that new scene. I didn't like the cloud of shame it spread over my life, and the darkness of it was hard to take at times. The only way I knew to camouflage my pain was by working harder and becoming a better provider. My ego continued to crumble under pressure, as grief was mapped on my heart. For the first time I was disappointed in myself, because things turned out differently than I anticipated. I could learn to be a better provider for my children; but could I prepare them for life's unexpected twists and turns; when I found myself lost in them? Then, I realized that no one could've prepared me for this journey. I had to learn something new as I went through each day, gently and obediently; trying to make it count the best way I knew how.   There were no shortcuts on this path; since it was the road less traveled by our family.   Quite honestly, I was not expecting great words of comfort.   But what I ended up with was a whole lot better: we simply didn't talk about it!

The newness of it was overwhelming so everyone decided to avoid the subject all together.   After all, there was a possibility that the estranged husband would come home, and the broken wife would reconcile with him.   None of those events happened.   I was determined to forge my own path as a single mother, and be the best that I could be.   A broken family is never a goal.   It is a heartbreak that bleeds internally, from the youngest to the oldest; until it is cauterized by the fiery darts of the unknown and the unexpected.   It is a curse in most cases.   And when the union becomes too toxic, one of the parties involved has to pull the plug in order to save the good that's left.   If the integrity of the relationship is too far gone, there could be more unbearable damage while trying to glue it together.   A greater tragedy is when two opposites stay in an unhappy marriage, and teach their children the wrong things about love.

I don't know how long it was before we started to feel safe and stable in our family of three we called our new normal.   Luckily, the transition took place without destroying our ability to move forward. As parents, we didn't wish each other ill.   At least I know I didn't. The focus was on the kids and their wellbeing.   The other pieces of the puzzle went to their proper place in due time.   Since this new journey was slow; we couldn't rush.

Brokenness entered my life through my mother whose idea of

discipline consisted of humiliation and shame.   She never knew how priceless my innocence was as a baby.   Her determination to establish dominance over me took away every bit of self-image as my future kept diminishing in size and magnitude; until someday, the person I could have become disappeared completely.   By then, all of my aspirations had vanished as well; leaving behind a deep and pervasive sadness, with a tendency toward self-destruction. Twenty-four years and two more marriages later, I now understand why I continued to make the same mistakes.   I was made to believe the injury was my fault.   I had played the role assigned to me by my abuser.   And I didn't know how to break that cycle, until I was given a greater purpose: I became a *Mom*.   This was quite an upgrade for me; and it gave me new level of determination to start over.

    I love helping people and I love giving them my hundred percent.   Often, I attract my complete opposite.   When I see someone's lacks and sorrows, I lend a sympathetic ear and listen to their problems.   I'm quite confident that a certain word of wisdom I might utter could encourage or even inspire them.   I don't expect anything in return, because this is not about exchanging goods.   It's about sharing with those who happen to be in need.   And it's never to reap eternal benefits either, as some of you may think.   When my listening, or my occasional advice helps someone or raises their self-esteem, it gratifies me and validates who I am, just like a customs officer validates a passport with a stamp.   I may neglect my own needs and feelings because I tend to be busy concentrating on others'. I may even step into their muddy situations out of concern; and encounter some unnecessary emotional issues.   But if I've made a difference at the end, I certainly sleep better at night.

It makes me feel good about who I am.

       Studies show that adult survivors of emotional abuse have two life-choices.   They either remain a victim, or they learn to self-reference; which is the case for me.   My greatest inheritance comes from my Dad.   It was his famous positive attitude that got me through each psychological event.   His love helped me catch my breath, and grow stronger.   I never quit believing I deserved love and respect.   And if those attributes weren't going to come my way naturally, I would earn them somehow.   I was also going to make sure my brother would never endure the negligence that challenged my childhood.   I wanted to be a lighthouse, and shine into the dark valleys of his life.   He didn't have to embrace the light; nor did he even need to appreciate it.   I simply wanted him to find his way to happiness with less struggle.   In fact, that's my prayer for everyone out there.   That's why I don't help people with just a few words.   I stay with them and encourage them until they reach the light at the end of their tunnel.   What could be more rewarding than seeing muddied individuals break free and soar, unbound for the rest of their journey?

CHAPTER 1.   ISTANBUL

I feel great this morning.   I didn't have to wake up to my alarm's infernal shouts.   And I didn't hit the snooze button several times either.   I get to stay home today.   It's my day off.   Being tightly bundled up in a robe after a shower took me back to Turkey where I grew up.   The government controlled all public utilities in those days.   They were allowed in certain subdivisions of the city during various intervals.   Having running water and the natural gas to heat it with, and the electrical power that generated the furnace, all at the same time, was a rare opportunity.   It usually took place after midnight within our neighborhood.   Mom and Dad had assigned one night a week - it had to be Friday since we didn't have school the next day - for us to stay up late and bathe properly.   My brother Jirayr and I looked forward to that cherished time of suds and bubbles, for however long it lasted.   It was a treat today's child would know nothing about.   To this day I appreciate this simple daily task of mine, knowing that it's still a huge privilege in many parts of the world.

There is much I would gladly forget about those years, but what is life without memories?   Isolating or altering them would make me a different person, perhaps in small but significant ways. I've learned to embrace them all, the good and the bad, because what makes me unique relies on sensations and impressions.   I especially love those that creep into my consciousness for no apparent reason, whisking me off to a land of yesteryears where I was simply passing through.   I see no harm in looking for my child self now and then. After all, it is her lessons of experience that shaped my taste-buds so I can savor today's simple moments.   I celebrate the courage she mustered up to let go of what she couldn't change, just so she can leave me with the glow of contentment I feel today.

As I pour hot coffee into a clean mug, I anticipate a well-deserved laziness this morning. Staring into the hallway mirror has become a habit lately. It helps me decompress. So I take the time. Studying my own reflection fascinates me. Not because I'm trying to see how many new wrinkles have flocked to their comrades. That's no longer a concern at my age. It's more like trying to detect traces of the original product; just as the expert analyzes the pentimento underneath an ancient, yet valuable painting. I just want to catch my reflection; the one I prefer to see sans makeup. Being a beautician over three decades, I know how to enhance certain features and look more polished. However, the ritual of grooming is more about enhancing my daily mood. I tend to wear a heavier makeup on the days I feel a bit depressed. Yet on my day off, seeing the true *me* is quite comforting. Many things keep changing. I yearn for something familiar.

The tired face echoing back from the mirror troubles me for a minute. Her countenance offers limited expression. Though her aged and somber reflection suggests she'd rather be left alone; I can tell she wants to connect. I know her; but her stares of disappointment are in the way. I shut my eyes for a few seconds hoping to recall a less tattered image of her. I inhale deep and trace every line left behind. Her fading silhouette is like a smoke vanishing into thin air. I try to memorize. I want to reach her before she departs. She holds the key to my untold stories. My unlived dreams are entrusted to her for the time being. She's the window of my soul.   She's got to preserve the warmth of my yesterdays, when innocence was priceless.   Her secrets determine my fate.   She has to survive!   My attempts to catch a glance of her dissipate quickly.   I open my eyes.   I let her go.

    I pull away from the mirror, walk into my cozy little den, and nestle gingerly among the cushions of my favorite sofa.   With fingers interlocked firmly around the hot liquid, I feel peace.   I've set aside this moment for a glorious visit with "moi".   How long has it been since I've had the pleasure?   I don't recall.   My life is hectic.   I'm extremely busy.   I've taken many detours from serenity which is a huge luxury these days.   Even though I acknowledge the need, it's a rare occasion.   If anything, I'm always looking back and refereeing past incidents.   "Was I too quick to judge?", "Did I give it a fair chance?", or "Should I've said it differently?" are my usual thoughts of self-examination.   I love being with myself every now and then.   It suggests a level of anticipated joy.   It's entirely different than being by myself, which sounds boring.

    This morning, departing from the present for a little while is an invitation I can't refuse.   I have the time to visit some childhood memories.   And there's so much to remember!   You see, I joined the refugee communities within the United States about thirty-five years ago.   Starting over isn't for sissies.   I had to walk away from an identity I could no longer have.   Treasures of before had to be buried.   Memories were painful.   So I tucked them in, hoping they'll awake later.   This process varies for each person.   It's a journey of defiance and dare; because what each individual leaves behind is entirely different.   Their personal goal is unique.   Their ability to cope with the unpredictable hasn't been challenged enough.   Nor can they foresee the hand they'll be dealt.   Not everyone receives a high card by suit.   Results are always uncertain.   For many, it's the last throw of the dice!

      I am of Armenian heritage, born and raised in Istanbul, where many of my early introductions to life, as well as my personal interpretations of it took place.   There are great many details about Istanbul I'll always miss.   To me, it's a lot more than just geography and history, domes and minarets.   It's a patch on the global atlas where the old and the new has managed to converge ever so gracefully.   Even though cross-cultural studies have revealed opposites don't mix well, Istanbul is where West meets East with vibrancy and charm.   I'm yet to speak to a visitor who didn't fall in love with this magical city.

      The smell of the fresh coffee calls my attention.   Just one swallow of it gives me a floating sensation.   Its warmth sooths my inner chambers until I'm at a place of leisure; away from everything. I'm plunging into the depths of my restful destination.   I shut my eyes to savor the full bodied flavor as it wafts into my taste buds, and visualize the farmers who catered to the rows of plants, as they meticulously planned everything.   They hoped for the right climate. They prayed for the right amount of rainfall at the right time. Securing a bountiful harvest was vital for their existence.   It was their life!   Not only am I tasting the result of their hard work now; but I'm also cheering the teamwork; as if I've labored with them all along! What a delight!

I also enjoy the fact that I don't have to impress anyone with my coffee. Preparing a small cup of Turkish coffee is tedious work. I remember when prospective husbands and their entourage judged a young lady's merits based on the taste of her coffee. Even the way she carried herself while placing the tiny cup into each individual's hand without any nervous tremor was an important detail to notice. One small mistake could be interpreted as lack of discipline or lack of proper upbringing; both highly embarrassing for the parents.

I admire the home and family dynamics the most. People invited anyone over to their house for breakfast or even dinner. Removing shoes before entering the premises was mandatory. The guests would receive a pair of slippers. Hospitality was very important. It was okay to follow the lady into her kitchen and help her prepare the meal while men sat in the living room and carried a conversation. Age and rank among family members were never forgotten. Disrespect towards an elder was unforgivable. Tending to the needs of an elder, whether it be family or not, was always a priority. People valued their homes. They took good care of their furnishings since replacing them wasn't easy. Ladies were always making little doilies to protect the tables and the armrests. They took pride in how organized and spotless their home was before the men arrived after work.

Two suspension bridges across the Bosphorus - the Bosphorus Bridge and the Fatih Sultan Mehmet Bridge, also known as the Bosphorus Bridge II, were built to connect the two lands of Istanbul. The appearance is majestic. More people prefer the European side because of its historic importance. It's also the city's commercial center with banks, stores, corporations, and two-thirds of its population.   My memory brings street merchants trying to dodge government officers.   The constant honking of aggressive drivers. The cussing and declaring of frustrated pedestrians.   And kids begging for money at street corners.   I wished we lived on the Asian side where my aunt and her husband did.   That part of Istanbul was more relaxed, with wide boulevards, residential neighborhoods, and fewer hotels.   I loved visiting them during the Spring break.   They were wealthy.   They owned their own business. They lived in a newer building with parquet floors, and a bathtub.   Soaking and playing with bubbles "during the day" were the highlights of my visit.   They didn't have kids.   And my brother Jirayr wasn't old enough to stay with me. So I was the only child for a whole week.   I milked it! Though unpredictable and occasionally dangerous, Istanbul is still the largest city in Turkey.   It's the fifth largest in the world by population yet the only one that occupies two different continents.   The Bosphorus strait, the 31Km long waterway, forms a natural boundary between its Asian and European sides.   It also connects the Black Sea with the Sea of Marmara.   It presents an awesome view where most of the finer hotels and restaurants cater to their patrons.   Live entertainment and belly dancers accompany the world renowned Turkish cuisine.   And as long as our parents had Raki at the table - which is Turkish Ouzo - everything tasted and sounded divine.   Of course the table had to be adorned with multiple appetizers - mezzes.   I was dad's dance partner since mom didn't care to dance.   I also enjoyed those occasional Saturday nights when we went out to dinner and watched live entertainment.   And dad would park the car by the boardwalk after dinner, facing the sea and the Asian shore, just so we could have ice cream while adults took in the beauty.   Those were sporadic and exceptional outings for us. But to a tourist, I'm certain they would be quite enchanting.

To think that Istanbul had been continually inhabited as a bridge between continents, as well as several civilizations, is quite a mystery. Excavations reveal finds dating back to the third millennium, BC on both sides. As the capital of the Roman Empire, the Byzantine Empire, and the Ottoman Empire, this fortified city was famed for its massive defenses. Although besieged on numerous occasions by various kingdoms, it was recovered in 1261 by the Byzantine Emperor Michael VIII Palaiologos, at which time its architectural masterpieces were cathedrals and palaces for its' Greek population. The Hagia Sophia was an Orthodox Cathedral which served as the seat of the Ecumenical Patriarchate. The sacred Imperial Palace, the Galata Tower, the Hippodrome, and the Golden Gate lined the arcaded avenues and squares until the Ottoman Sultan Mehmed II conquered the city in 1453. Istanbul, former Constantinople, was almost depopulated until it regained its reputation as the largest city of the Ottoman Empire in the mid 1600's.

In 1915, Turks set in motion a plan to expel and massacre Armenians, about 2 million that lived within the Ottoman Empire. By the early 1920's, when the atrocities and deportations finally ended, some 1.5 million of Turkey's Armenians were dead, or forcibly removed from the country. Today this event is called Genocide, a premeditated and systematic campaign to exterminate an entire people. The materialization of *my* ancestry is within the remnants of that horrific tragedy. My grandmother, Guluzar, at age 12, watched the slaughtering of her entire family. A neighbor of theirs at the time, a good hearted Muslim man, hid her from the soldiers. I'll never understand how she managed to bury her pain, then marry a man twice her age, my grandfather, who also lost his entire family. She never spoke of that event, because, despite pressure from Armenians and social justice advocates throughout the world, it is still illegal in Turkey to talk about what happened to Armenians during this era. Grandma must have been a woman of faith. Otherwise she couldn't have dealt with the insanities of her life without harboring hatred and bitterness. Yet she died at age seventy-eight, peacefully, and happy to go home. Humility carried her where neither strength nor reason would prevail. The moment of her final breath was when good overcame evil eternally.

Genocide didn't get rid of us. It pushed us to different parts of the world. The end of the 1980's and the beginning of the 1990's were considered to be years of revival through the Armenian Apostolic Church in different parts of the Armenian society. It's no surprise that Armenians have always been targeted throughout the centuries because they were the first nation to adopt Christianity. And to this day Christianity is still an inherent part of the Armenian identity. In fact, the culture laid heavy stress on certain religious facts, so the words "Christian", "first", and "unique" are embedded in the core of Armenian mentality. Aside from the religious elements; history, culture, and education are primary forces that continue to form the important history of the Armenian people.

Today's Armenians abide by their heritage all over the world. Those little islands of cultural values form the Armenian nation. Most of us actively fight to support what's left behind. Our goal is to ensure a peaceful coexistence of our old traditions with our new reality; because we want to be integrated into the worldwide globalization process without losing our national identity.

Not only did we survive: we also persevered. How could we not? We have a moral obligation towards those who suffered and died during Genocide. And we have much to prove to the world. We've already seen terrorism doesn't work! Our history celebrates those who were determined to carry the torch of righteousness. This is one attribute of God that genetically keeps us in relationship with Him. It indicates our actions and intentions are justified in a pleasing way to God. When we dilute our values, we sabotage our strength and fortitude. And that hinders the distinct communication we have with Him. That is, of course, if we believe in the true living God. Otherwise righteousness is a self-serving hypocrisy and bigotry. My people's scars are deep enough to know where the right values emanate from, and not to ever cross that fine line between humility and pride.

Forgiving the past can be challenging for many. Only the sufferer is qualified to make that decision. Being able to find happiness regardless of the blunders and absurdities of yesterday is what makes life meaningful. It's far more than merely existing or overcoming obstacles. It's about taking each episode as a miracle, and amassing precious data that is meant to be used as a serious restore point someday. I believe my negative experiences taught me to treasure the simpler things in life as if they were ice cream sundaes - or *baklava* in my case. I still want more out of life; and I refuse to feel discouraged; just because I didn't always have the best of circumstances.

    I'm grateful for the changes that allowed my ancestors to coexist with the Islamic mentality in a rather subtle and peaceful way. In 1923 the Republic of Turkey replaced the old regime.   Mustafa Kemal, a decorated army officer, became its first president.   In 1928 he allowed the Latin alphabet to replace the Arabic, outlawed the veil, and gave women the voting rights.   He was a man with great vision whose march in the direction to a contemporary civilization is highly revered by everyone.   In 1934 he was granted the surname Ataturk, meaning "Father of the Turks."   Though the forces of temporary political lapses are still being felt by many, the tourism is at its best these days.   The only area of concern is over religious differences. Istanbul's natives possess great respect for their religious customs. People in open clothes will feel a bit uncomfortable; as they certainly are denied access to mosques and public institutions.   Isis is no greater threat in Istanbul than in any other major capital in the world.

    Though glad to have a stable life outside Turkey, I miss Istanbul's colorful markets.   I'm sure most migrants do, not only for the shopping experience, but also for the socializing.   Primarily designed for the tourists, The Grand Bazaar was one of the largest and oldest covered markets in the world.   It housed thousands of shops, detailed with intricate designs of mosaic-style tiles.   Jirayr and I were awestruck by the brave usage of bright colors and patterns while mom and dad searched for bargains.   The size of the Bazaar was overwhelming; it seemed to go on forever, it was filled with booths stocked high of tea and spices, rugs, jewelry and much memorabilia.

We learned at a young age not to appear interested.   That would've robbed us of getting a better deal from the merchants.   Bartering was an art in Istanbul.   I'm sure it still is.   Offering the smallest price without insulting the seller, is something we developed over time and experience.   When we walked past a store or restaurant entrance we heard expressions of courtesy.   The host always welcomed the passersby to grace his premises with their presence.   Walking away without a nod was disrespectful.   Acknowledging them and smiling back was a ritual we didn't overlook.

There was magic in the air when we heard the leader of prayers invite the inhabitants to the mosques five times a day.   I still remember the chaos of an overcrowded city where a sea of people was constantly churning every which direction; almost in a never-ending manner.   Not much of any rule was being followed.   A pedestrian-unfriendly traffic gave the wizardry of ruthless drivers an unfair advantage.   Just the thought of having to run for our lives in order to cross a street still makes my skin crawl.   Life might have been of a lesser value where a majority of the people suffered from a lack of education and governmental support, thus economic growth.
Feeding hungry mouths in a society that didn't allow women to invade the work force was arduous indeed.   Most children were looked upon as a burden; until they would grow up to become responsible contributors to their households; setting aside the need to start a family of their own.   The youngest of the family often inherited this huge responsibility; since leaving parents unassisted generated shame and guilt related responses.

I can't forget the lining up against one another within a city bus, swaying forward and then backward like a pendulum, each time the bus came to a sudden stop.   And more often than not, it did roll to a halt for unexpected and unforeseen reasons; allowing pickpockets and sexual predators an overwhelming benefit over their victims. Jumping in a clapped out old taxi for a long ride through the choking traffic would've been the other choice; along which came the pleasure of having overcome a terrifying cab ride.   The smallest details of this great metropolis were story-worthy adventures we shared over dinner with family members at the close of each day.   Safety was a byproduct of good fortune.   It needed to be celebrated every night.

    The lack of certain necessities such as bread and butter led to snakelike lines outside the grocery stores.   The controlled distribution of utilities was intolerable during the harsh winter months.   Nice neighborhoods were surrounded by dilapidated slums; making it hard to walk through without taking a chance.   Social inequality gave rise to instability and conflict all throughout this city with a bad boy appeal. The educational and intellectual background of its individuals, not just wealth or lack of it, gave birth to an unfairness within their social status and political power; leading them to collective actions.   Do I look back in wonder or do I shake my head in disbelief?   Did I truly enjoy living in that extraordinary place, or did I barely survive it? Only time would have those answers for me.

    Even though opportunities were limited in Istanbul, we were a part of the privileged crowd.   Our living standards were higher than average; thanks to our dad's hard work.   We lived in better neighborhoods and attended private schools.   We were sheltered from all sorts of violations, as well as violence itself.   Like many

Middle-Eastern countries, racism and ethnic discrimination is highly institutional against the non-Muslim minorities. It may have been possible for the Armenians to achieve status and wealth within the Ottoman Empire once upon a time. But now as a community, they are accorded a status as second-class citizens. Living in Turkey as a non-Muslim meant inefficiency, injustice in the courts, ungodly amounts of taxes, and the ignorance of corrupt officials. Trying to stay out of trouble and keeping a low profile were the simplest ways of surviving the system. And by the grace of God, our family played that part very well; until we safely migrated to America. Land of the free!

    The social precautions were confusing to us kids. Outside the school premises, cultural and religious differences separated us all. We were to be away from one another. We couldn't mingle. We couldn't even talk on the phone. That never made any sense to me! The answers were the same: "Why do you have to question everything?", or "That's not for you to know!" Those answers applied to political and traditional issues. I even got a, "Shh! They might hear you!" every now and then. I must admit, I had an inquiring mind. But I never got a straight answer to anything. I was left at the mercy of my ignorance. I still don't know how slapping a girl who got her first period entered an Armenian family. It was supposed to be a Jewish custom, known as Mazel Tov slap, carried out to regard the female body, its fertility, and its blood as shameful and potentially evil. So was staying away from a rising dough, because menstruating would've kept the bread from rising, or turned the wine sour. Why did we only inherit certain traditions? Where did the silver candlesticks and the prayer shawls ended up going? Could it be that the entrance into womanhood was a sign for a lifelong trouble, and not just the pending curves?   Or were we to be reminded that womanhood was the beginning of being reduced into a second class citizen in that culture?   I don't want to get into that!

    Most likely, nobody was given a chance to challenge the old beliefs.   Obscurities and superstitions were passed down because no one had the courage to question them.   Bruising the moral stamina was less important than angering ancestors.   That's why God remained a complete blur to me for a long time.   He was a tangled perception of my imagination.   First of all, He couldn't wait to punish me.   He despised disobedience.   He didn't tolerate noise.   He didn't even like loud laughter.   "Stop!   Those stupid giggles of yours will bring down God's punishment, you'll see!" I would hear often.   To me, God had become a flogging stick that came out of nowhere.   I was afraid of Him.   How could I know that He was being used as a means to discipline kids?   Obviously, those we looked up to had very little to no understanding of who God truly was.   Delicate details of our souls are formed by people who have been in charge of our upbringing.   They teach us the basics: our sense of responsibility, good and bad habits, and the ability to cope with difficulties.   The bright memories of our childhood strengthen us during trying times. But if we haven't had a decent start; in no way can we have a do over. Therefore, the possibility of having an intimate relationship with God someday never crossed my mind.   If anything, I always watched my back; because He was constantly watching me.

    Have you ever thought of the countless iniquities we inherit from those who form our mental and spiritual dimensions?   No wonder finding a correct path would be a great challenge for some of us!   As innocent adolescents, we snatch our parents' unresolved issues as if they were batons during a relay race.   As we take off running, we start receiving a few personal revelations such as... a track is nowhere to be found! ...we don't know which direction and how far to run! ... and there are no medals to be had at the end!   Yet we've been driven with the idea of some kind of a competition.   We've got to find it!   We must win something!   We go the extra mile!   We add a few twists and turns of our own; because walking away empty-handed means "defeat".   And defeat contaminates "self".   Our ego is very important.   It traps us in our own little world; all concerned of ruining who we aim to become.   It can make or break our psychological stability.   And mine is extremely fragile.

  Since I was uprooted for an entirely different lifestyle, the need to belong to something or to someone became important.   It was a huge necessity like food and shelter.   I'm pretty certain a great majority would agree with me.   For some it's a family.   For others it may be their office or their church.   The landscape of belonging may differ from one individual to another; but the importance of it is the same for everyone.   We're attracted to individuals with similar interests.   Our behavioral, emotional, and intellectual attributes draw us to certain characteristics.   So trying to juggle two different identities growing up was very confusing to say the least.

  We spoke Turkish almost all the time, unless when we were home.   We were to speak in Armenian behind closed doors.   Education was important in Istanbul.   Most everyone aimed to learn at least a second language.   I knew college wasn't in the cards for me.   Most girls were expected to get married and start a family after high school. But I still made good grades. They were important to Mom. She wasn't happy unless I made straight-A's. She demanded the best so she could brag to friends and family members. She didn't believe in motivational speeches though. Encouragement wasn't necessary. "Bringing good grades is the least you can do", she kept saying. And I was obedient to her demands. Thankfully, I loved studying. It was easy for me. I didn't care much for social studies; but I was great in math and science. Jirayr wasn't as fortunate. He needed a tutor due to his lack of concentration. I felt bad for him. I still remember him sitting on Dad's lap on the eve of every school year and crying. And Dad played with his hair while whispering sweet words of encouragement into his ears. I didn't need any of that. I was ready to go back to school. I came alive there. I could be me, and not an extension of Mom.

I was a talker. I couldn't button up and stop entertaining the class behind the teacher's back. Even my favorite teacher got tired of my disrupting the class one day. She made me write my crime on a piece of paper and attached it to my back. I was to walk up and down the hallways with that paper. That did slow me down a bit; but it didn't cure me completely. I simply learned to be a little more careful with my timing; that's all. But my grades were fabulous. I was brilliant. Most likely my talkative nature was a display of my boredom; because classes were too easy.

Once school was in recess for the summer months, we moved to an island called Kinali; one of the nine small islands known as the Prince Islands. They were located within the Sea of Marmara. The history reveals that in medieval times, those were the sites of monasteries, away from the temptations of the city. However, with the advent of steamships and ferryboat services, some of those islands turned into summer resorts. Though I didn't know how my parents juggled to afford the resort; my vibrant anticipation each spring displayed my gratitude.

    The island life was wonderful. Almost everyone knew one another, because the same group of people planned to reunite after a hard winter. And there was also a handful of residents that never left for the city. The cottage on the island was their only home. They endured the frigid winds of the cold months. But the summer breeze was worth the wait, delivering the amazing aroma of honeysuckle, gardenia, and all sorts of fragrant shrubbery. Carefully tucked in among those were tiny little vineyards. I only knew they were needed to make stuffed grape leaves; a delicacy most everyone enjoyed. Small and uncluttered homes of unique architecture were painted with vibrant colors. They completed the dazzling display of sunsets overlooking the crystal-blue sea. Though slightly pricier compared to the city, grocery stores as well as fruit and vegetable stands along the curbs catered to everyone's needs. And if we were to hike the hills in order to take in the entire panoramic view, we reached a magnificent monastery that sat majestically in a wooded area. Resting underneath a tree, while a gentle breeze caressed our cheeks felt like a piece of heaven.

    At least that's how I envisioned heaven then. Today I believe it's a place for rest, without any darkness; therefore, without a sun and a moon. The Creator's glory is the only source of illumination, spreading its warmth and peace, wisdom and knowledge; and attracting arrivers who are there to celebrate a life well lived.   And since there is no need for a source of heat and light, there's very little or no gravity; without which there could be no waters.   The river of life flowing from the throne of God is not liquid water as we know it. I was once immersed in it during a vision.   What appeared to be zillions of diamonds covering its entire surface glistened under the radiance of indescribably intense light that should've blinded me.   But it was comfortable to stare at.   It was mesmerizing.   It had all of the properties of an ocean.   It cooled me off; yet I stepped out of it completely dry.   I don't know why I was given a glimpse of heaven a few years back.   It certainly was quite a display.   It showed me what I could miss if I weren't being careful with my choices.   I don't believe I'm an exception.   I see myself less than average.   But I believe in the extraordinary God in a highly stubborn way.   I'm quite confident that if I had stayed in Turkey, many of the awakenings I've been fortunate enough to receive wouldn't have reached me, due to the negative notions I was fed on.   That's probably why I enjoyed climbing the rough terrain of that monastery as often as I could where serenity was tangible.   I felt right at home there.

   The island was known to be safe.   No one ever worried about their kids not making it home at night.   The doors didn't need to be locked.   Often we stayed on the beach until it was time to get cleaned up and get ready for the evening ritual.   This customary daily practice consisted of almost all families parading up and down the main boardwalk, looking their best, until their breadwinner would step out of the ferryboat navigating between the city and the islands.   And if he didn't, his family continued the promenade until the next ferry arrived.   There was no returning home until the provider made it back safely to the island.

Each time I managed to see Dad emerge from the crowd of travelers I would be filled with a sense of pride. He stood out. To me he was the best looking one, the strongest, and the kindest. I was honored to be his daughter. I remember running to hug him with open arms as if I hadn't seen him for a long while. He smiled back and held me against his chest while Jirayr tried to climb up into his other arm. We weren't complete until our daddy was home.

Sitting around the dinner table and listening to our parents talk about the everyday stuff was comforting. Occasionally Dad asked how our day had been. This was the ultimate satisfaction for both of us. Jirayr and I raced to get in as many words as possible. Giving an account of our day was a privilege. After all, "kids were to be seen; and not heard" in that part of the world. But Dad always included us. We longed for the weekends when he was home. We wouldn't leave him alone. Our greatest pleasure was to join him in bed while he read us the comic page. He doubled over with laughter. And more often than not, he couldn't finish reading, because we would be all over him, wrestling and having fun. His contagious laughter was all it took.

Fishing was Dad's favorite hobby. Him and his brother spent hours on their boat. We could barely see them on the horizon as a straight line and two dots. They would be gone for hours but they never came home empty handed. They had more than enough. They shared their catch with fellow neighbors. It was always abundant. A true fisherman is known for his courage to brave the deep sea, his ability to overcome disappointments without trying new or more deadly lures, and his patience to mend the fishing nets before the next trip. Dad was all smiles no matter how arduous the task.

Dad's other pastime was to play cards with his friends at a nearby coffee shop. We weren't allowed to go in. We could only peep through the window. A pervading sense of comfort penetrated us each time we saw him smile back. We belonged to him! Through him, we experienced the true essence of life: the unconditional love of a parent who would do anything for us. He was amazing! He gave us the things he never had. He was a grade school dropout. Both he and his younger brother apprenticed at their grandfather's carpentry shop. They had to help out with household expenses; while their sister stayed home with their mother. She needed to learn how to be a homemaker. By the time grandma got done with her, my aunt was an excellent cook and a seamstress. She designed and made all of her dresses. She looked amazing. She was quite a lady. She would marry wealthy someday, and never have to work. And that she did! Dad and his brother took on the carpentry profession as expected. They made a good team. There never were any arguments between them. They appreciated each other's strengths. Dad was good at managing employees, while my uncle negotiated with other business owners. Together they walked the business into its most successful stages.

I never wore a headscarf back in Istanbul; but the thought of a towel tightly wrapped around my head takes me there every time. I walk into the kitchen to refill my cup, and fix myself a piece of toast for breakfast. I remember the freshly baked bread we used to buy daily for our meals. It had a thick crust and smelled good.   Often we broke big chunks of it before it even made it to the table where most of our entertainments took place.   "I must be getting hungry!" I think to myself.   I'm fighting the aroma of the pastries that once adorned our table. The Turkish cuisine was colorful with its abundant use of vegetables, nestled next to a lamb, beef, chicken, or seafood. The grilling of the meat was in the form of kebabs, mainly on skewers, garnished with rice pilaf.   And no spread was ever complete without some feta cheese and Turkish black olives.   Though poverty was highly visible in large cities, most everyone in Istanbul could afford "the fish bread".   It was a popular sandwich.   And it was delicious.   Dad loved it.   Thinking of him brings another smile to my heart. Memories of him renew me every time.   It's as if I rediscover myself. Dad and I were as two peas in a pod. I miss him...

I don't always like my catch in the sea of memories, but I like going for a dip now and then.   Each treasure brings a level of understanding to the mystery of life.   It becomes the missing piece to my puzzle. With a little luck, I'll swim deep enough and make a triumphant exit with some new goods from the past.   They will keep me preoccupied for a while; until the urge to dive for more strikes again.   Memories stimulate me philosophically and spiritually.   How else can I fully understand my life lessons and categorize them properly?   They help me develop appreciation.   What's the sense in doing better and having more if I don't know to appreciate it? Gratitude shaped Jirayr and me as young kids.   It went beyond good manners.   We were told, "If you remain grateful, life will bring you many blessings."   We weren't allowed to complain, or act entitled. Both led to punishment.   We were to learn how interdependent everyone was. We needed to know and care where things came from. Family rules were not to be taken lightly. Altering them was an insult. Our priorities were set out for us with   reminders of the sacrifices our parents made.

Dad always had something kind to say. His words were uplifting. He appreciated my good grades. He was proud of my hard work. Even though I enjoyed being at the top of my class, seeing a smile on his face was the icing on the cake. That was my way of doing something for him. Being absent for the most part and expected to fulfill our material needs, Dad was busy earning money. Financial decisions and household repairs were his domain. He operated a woodworking shop where he employed about a dozen workers. He made furniture. He knew lumber and all of its attributes. He selected the right kind of wood for each project. He had inherited the profession from his great-grandfather who happened to be the only carpenter of his time. Our apartment was furnished with handmade items. I'll never forget the smell of freshly cut lumber, set aside to adapt to climate changes, before it was ready to be formed into something new. Jirayr and I played with the remnants. We built cities with parking garages and airports, and used every piece to suit our imagination. We didn't need toys; nor could we even afford any. Our creative thinking and fantasies helped us leap from one idea to another; making each one the reality of that moment. We didn't allow the bigotry and the senseless incriminations the previous generations had been subjected to. We made sure our world was a happy one!

Dad's strong work ethic was inherent in that part of the world where political and socioeconomic unrest shadowed everyone's financial stability.   His strength and leadership taught Jirayr and me how to yield to the needs of those under our care.   Neither of us would expect a "thank you" for the provisions we offer our children. We both consider our moral obligations as God-given responsibilities. We take pride in supplying them with our best.   Our dedication is also our strength.   Watching Dad offered us good qualities.   We were drawn to him because he was happy and loving.   He didn't need to preach.   In fact, he never did.   He simply played the part well.   He made it into a fun game; and not a dread.   As far as I'm concerned, Jirayr and I are still each other's best friend, just like Dad and his siblings were.

     I notice the time on the DVD player beneath the television set. It's 1:37 already.   And I've been sitting here for hours reliving my childhood.   I am satisfied with the bittersweet memories of today's visit.   The dreadful ones I could do without.   I'm sure they'll surface sooner or later, and sprinkle their temporary gloom.   But today I cherish the peaceful state I'm in.   In fact, it's time to get up and tackle some household chores before the day is over.   The bedroom is a mess.   Standing by the doorjamb, I murmur, "Something has to be done".   Piles of clothes have been accumulating for three weeks. I'm going to address this problem first!   Otherwise I'll have to move into the guest-bedroom.   That may sound funny but I've done it before.   It didn't help.   I ended up with a bigger mess to sort out. That's why I'm not going to let the clutter intimidate me today.   These rags are going to be put away.   I feel like a snail; except my trail is colorful.   I mumble as I sort my garments into smaller piles.   I know talking to my clothes sounds creepy; but I can't help it.   I need to be heard.   It'll remain my little secret as long as I don't talk back.

Often I let my household chores accumulate.   I don't have a routine.   I don't like monotony.   I like focusing on projects.   They distract me from the occasional loneliness I feel; though loneliness is highly unbearable when I'm in a relationship.   If I meet someone I feel interested in; first, I'm convinced he's the right one.   I brag about the things we have in common.   I become the project manager.   I coordinate all sorts of fun stuff we could do together.   I plan all of the entertainments; until someday, I realize *I'm* the entertainment.   Making that person happy is my job.   Then as the relationship falters, I look for ways to tolerate the stranger I'm with; and the stranger I've become.   I heard a preacher say, "... it's better to want something you don't have than to have something you don't want!"   That sums it up for me.   My result is always the same: feeling stuck.   And I feel miserable each time!

My life is dreamy these days.   My imagination is at rest, because the peace I feel today comes from a fruitful spiritual growth. The more frequently I meditate, the more consummate is the peace within.   That's where fears and worries dissipate.   Fighting iniquity and focusing on good attributes is my goal.   I focus less on changing circumstances and more on mitigating their effects.   I've learned to take full responsibility for my own worth, instead of relying on others' opinions of me.   This keeps me from playing the victim.

Stress is an epidemic in today's world.   It harms our health. We don't even breathe properly when we worry about things we have little or no control over.   Stress is the root cause of many chronic and autoimmune disorders.   It contributes to inflammation, particularly in the coronary arteries, resulting in heart attacks.   It affects cholesterol levels.   Why do we invite its tyranny?   Why do we give it permission to settle into our lives?   I have prayed for peace many times in the past.   But just as soon as I would finish praying, chaos would enter! And after several similar episodes, I understood peace takes place within.   It has to grow and develop gradually.   So just as the flicker of a candle is appreciated in total darkness, I must light the wick of peace during turmoil, in order to find my way!   We can't buy peace; but we can certainly rely on it to preserve us while facing difficult situations.   With peace, it's possible to face an overdrawn bank account, or a betrayal by someone we care about, or even, wading into a messy bedroom without feeling overwhelmed.   There is a solution for every problem.   And the good news is, "problems are temporary", as long as we don't allow them to darken our lives.

   After starting a load in the washing machine, I take furniture polish and a few rags back to my room.   I'm ready to declutter the space.   Confusion will end.   I like privacy, and I like quiet.   But I *love* having order.   That love motivates me to fight!   Love is strength. I've used it to clear my spiritual clutter.   Once I realized God created me after His image, my worth could not be determined by an ill-minded upbringing.   I found hope.   I was important after all. That revelation showed me God's love for me.   His unconditional love healed my childhood wounds.   I realize I am precious.   I am incalculable.   I am God's composition!   And I am out-of-this-world! Put-downs and disappointments don't mar His creation.   I am worth the fight!

CHAPTER 2. DISASTER

I notice the dark clouds in the sky. They're huddled together vertically, which means we must be getting ready for a storm. The picturesque view is quite an indication of strong winds and possible heavy rain. Dad had taught me plenty about weather patterns; since he had to watch the signs before he went fishing. He would say, "If there is a halo round the sun or moon, then we can all expect rain quite soon." My personal studies as a teenager proved that this was true. A ring would form around the moon due to high altitude clouds, commencing low-pressure systems bearing moisture. He also believed, "When grass is dry in the morning light, look for rain before the night." Again, a true statement. Dew forms only on clear and still nights. So when the grass has no dew in the morning, it usually means the wind has picked up during the night, with the possibility of dark cloud formations. His favorite was, "Red sky at night, sailor's delight. Red sky in the morning, sailor's warning." The red clouds in the morning would typically be in the west and heading towards us; whereas red clouds at night would be in the east, having passed us by.

Studying the clouds became a hobby of mine not just because of Dad's teachings; but also because I was deathly afraid of storms. Yet the thought of it today paints a smile on my face. "What a perfect day to stay in", I mumble. I haven't been following the weather center lately. I used to be obsessed with it. I would be glued to the television set, wanting to absorb all of the latest details. Running to the nearby grocery store to stuck up on food wouldn't even cross my mind. Most refugees don't worry about food and water so much. They learn to make do with less.

I still don't know if my fear had anything to do with my misconceptions about God. I was taught to believe all bad things happened in this world as a punishment from Him. His fury against human disobedience would cause nature to spin out of control, and bring on devastations such as droughts, earthquakes, thunders and lightning. My heartbeat would start to get intense during the rumbling in the distance; but as the thunderclaps reached their loudest stages, I would curl up in a corner, shaking and crying. Lightning in particular were the most frightening. I didn't care about appliances. I was worried about having done something awful that deserved huge penance.

We arrived in Virginia in the Spring of 1980. I researched the area and its climate. It all sounded very promising until one day residents were preparing for something called a "hurricane". I didn't know what that word meant. I kept asking with my broken English. Most likely I didn't want to get it; because their sign language was describing a storm. I was being introduced to Hurricane Gloria of 1985 that ended up devastating our street with uprooted trees that landed on parked vehicles or on the rooftops. I had never seen anything like that before. Friends had given me instructions to go to a nearby shelter, not knowing I didn't have a way to get there. All I could do was hug my two kids, three and seven then, and chant a prayer that went on for hours. We were all dressed in our street clothes in case we lost our home. That sounds pretty dumb now; considering I was afraid we weren't going to survive this horrendous storm.

I can't mention Gloria without bringing up Hurricane Isabel of

2003. This one made Gloria look like an amateur. Isabel was the costliest disaster in the history of Virginia, with winds of 165mph. It downed thousands of trees, leaving behind 1.85 billion in damage, and 36 deaths in the state. Where was I during all that? I had stepped out into the backyard, admiring the powerful clouds, with my arms stretched out as if I wanted to caress them. My phobia had left me between husband number one and husband number three by then. A heavy rainfall signified the washing and the sanctification of the soul. I couldn't be bothered with dismembered tree limbs and branches. They were tiny details compared to my personal cleansing process. I had stopped fearing hurt or danger. A storm was as natural to me as a sunshiny day. Its landscape may have been slightly different: no sunshine. Isn't it marvelous that bad things don't last? Good always prevails. Time and patience have witnessed it.

My three marriages could be discussed in one chapter; mainly because neither qualifies for one of its own. That would be a waste of my time and yours. They had one thing in common: to dominate. Each husband was attracted to my independence as well as my intelligence; yet each needed a less of an independent and intelligent woman to feel good about himself. And all I wanted was to belong and be a portion of a good man. I was brought up to agree and accept. I was simply looking for a husband who would be the head of my household, without trying to take advantage of my submissive upbringing.

Finding the courage to walk away from toxic situations hasn't been a problem so far; but I've always needed to hibernate for a while, and get my thinking straight afterwards. I had to free myself from all of their negativities. I refuse to walk around with anger and bitterness. That's not who I am. If I've allowed someone to mistreat me, that also means I've played a part. I want to own that responsibility, and move forward with peace and forgiveness. Not that I condone the bullying and the terrorizing of defenseless victims. Bad behaviors are never justifiable! But not being able to dismiss them could cause me to linger within their grip. It's a process needed for my healing; lest I chance remaining the victim a lot longer than I'm willing. My biggest advice for my children has always been, "do not exhaust yourself trying to change the world you live in; see to it that it doesn't change you!"

Anger is a byproduct of an ongoing unfairness, numerous broken promises, or shattered dreams of a "happily ever after" intent. It's a God-given reaction that comes natural to us all; as long as we don't get stuck in it. If handled poorly, anger that motivates us to leave a dangerous relationship can also cause us to attack the abusive party, dragging us into an even more volatile retaliation. Though it's never easy, for me the best answer is to walk as fast as I can, and not look back; until a resting place is found. Once anger has propelled me out of an abusive situation, it's no longer useful. Its primary reason for being is over and done with. I try not to let it spread roots and cause bitterness; which is a result that could only exalt my oppressor. The need to be angry starts dissipating when I start letting go of the victim identity. Recognizing its symptoms is a huge accomplishment. Even when the awareness sets in, it still takes me a long time to admit "I'm being abused". And it takes purposeful determination to focus on the fact that "I'm entitled to be treated decently by others."

Getting hurt for the sake of sharing my life with someone is not acceptable.

Being someone's punching bag is never okay. There is never a good reason for any one person to physically or emotionally beat on another person. Humiliations and degradations have reduced me in the past; but at the end I always manage to say, "It's your loss." Living well is my revenge. Forgiveness towards the abusers is possible; but it shouldn't be forced. It happens on its own time. And one thing is for certain, "Having been abused is never a good enough excuse one should use to abuse others.

It's taken me years to dissect and figure out why things didn't work out for me. I now understand a great majority of people confuse meekness with weakness, kindness with stupidity, and mercy with mutism. I was brought up to weigh my words and think before I speak. I still do. Once out there, words travel far deeper into hearts, and live longer than our mere existence here on earth; especially those spoken in anger. More irreparable damages occur with one ill sentence that cannot be taken back; nor can it be rephrased in order to pare down its harm. We must speak with caution and respect. That's part of being a civilized person.

Didn't we learn to wash our hands before eating, cover our mouth before sneezing, or say "please" and "thank you" when asking for something? Such statements taught us to be a part of our society. They're common sense rules. They'll always be important. Yet the following statement most of us grew up saying wasn't quite as accurate as it made us feel at the time: "Sticks and stones may break my bones, but words will never hurt me."   To be honest, I'd rather have a broken bone or two than to have endured the pain of unkind and belittling words I've heard over the years.   I wish I could forget them.   They're not haunting me every moment of my life; but they're somewhere near and ready to decimate each progress I make.   I don't give into their solicitations.   They're no longer my problem.   I believe others will be held accountable for them some day.

Each husband pursued me as if he couldn't live without me.   And most likely he couldn't; but not because I was the answer to his prayers.   More like I was the clay he'd been needing to mold into something he would admire for a while, until some day he had the urge to smash it into pieces; just because he was having a bad day.   He didn't expect those fragments to have a negative reaction, because psychopaths don't believe they're ever wrong.   They have a grandiose self-perception.   They believe the sweet and pleasant mask they manage to wear out in public will afford them whatever they think they deserve, without paying a price.   And if they happen to appear remorseful for hurting you, it's only because they're preparing you to console them.   After all, in their selective perception, you're the one who caused them to behave badly.   And they hate stillness.   The minute you stop stimulating their ego, they've already turned on you. I'm not trying to discuss various aspects of a mental illness here.   I'm just pointing out the common denominators I found during my attempts for a healthy marriage.   Needless to say, I'm able to spot pathological tendencies a lot easier and also identify them from afar these days.

But I never saw the threat they posed in my early adolescent years. I must've been familiar with their patterns. Men placed me on a pedestal. They held me high. They boasted about me every chance they had. But not because I was all that! Only because they were programming me to elevate their ego. I was to make them feel good! And I was to make them look good! Impaired by an abusive parent or two, those rotten seeds had been too weak to survive their own damages. "Monkey see, monkey do" was the only thing they had learned. Being pretentious was simply a facade to cover their scars. They couldn't live alone; because someone's good graces had to overshadow their own filthy opinion of themselves. And why did I attract those losers? It's simple. Because I too was broken at an early age! How we were parented during our formative years puts in place the choices we make and the partners we look for.

    I made poor choices. I didn't know how to pick. My ideas of what was right for me were distorted during my childhood years. I didn't know my worth, because I had none. Mom's life would've been a lot simpler if I had followed her biddings. "If only you would do as told!" She shook her head with contempt every time she uttered those words. I don't know why I questioned things for which she had no answers. I guess I had an inquiring mind. I didn't mean to challenge her intelligence when she was barely making it as a parent. I thought I was supposed to look up to her for issues I couldn't figure out on my own. I was wrong. Mom had a preassigned idea for my future. So she had to reduce me for it. She was trying to fit me into a smaller box. I wasn't tall enough to become a stewardess. I wasn't smart enough to become a teacher. I could never work outside the house. What would the neighbors think?

Mom continued to plant all the wrong seeds, and Dad didn't have the courage to step in. He gave in to her ways. He let her be. It was easier that way. Instead, he nursed me back to health with seeds of "optimism". He wasn't being the kind of hero I would've wanted him to be at the time. But he was sharing something with me he could afford without being obvious. He helped me develop a mindset that served me a lifetime. Dad's love was free-flowing. I never questioned it. He also loved his wife. He was determined to make his marriage work. He used weapons such as kindness and gentleness Mom knew nothing about; just so he could override her troubled approach to life's ordinary circumstances. As a family, we appeared healthy. No one ever knew we were missing some of the most important boundaries. Our huge secret was sacred; because for Mom, how something looked was far more important than how it felt.

Did Dad know bad decisions were going to follow me for the rest of my adult life? Was he trying to prepare me for them? Maybe. But even if he wasn't, he still ended up planting the kind of seeds I would've needed eventually. He was a good man with a good heart. I don't even know one positive adjective with which to describe Mom. She was more like lightning that caused major root damage below the ground, despite the absence of visible external symptoms. The heat and pressure waves she generated as she controlled everyone in the family were meant to destroy any attribute she saw as a threat. She had to rule everything. The depth and enormity of her power over me eventually became obvious; just not in time to help minimize its damages. However, Dad's presence and encouraging words kept me from collapsing like a necrotic plant. Mom was oblivious. She was the normal one! Not only would she create the defects in our family, but she would also hold us responsible for them; tormenting us with criticisms.

I was confused and disoriented because I couldn't make any sense of her interpersonal tricks and stunts. I disliked her for them. And I hated myself for feeling that way. I would've given anything to love her like friends of mine loved their Mom. I wanted to be able to trust her with my life, instead of having to hide from her wrath. As a result, I ended up internalizing shame and anger. I turned on myself. I kept thinking, "What's wrong with me?", "I'm such a failure!", or "I'm so stupid!" I was only as good as she said I was, and felt loved only if I was fully compliant with her wishes.

The rest is quite obvious, and almost inevitable. I felt like fish out of water in relationships where I was loved and cherished consistently. They seemed superficial to me; because I didn't grow up with the belief that I was intrinsically okay. I didn't believe I was worthy of good. Therefore, I kept gravitating toward drama-laden, roller-coaster relationships. I attracted partners who were emotionally unavailable, critical, or withholding. I was programmed to be a scapegoat.

Most narcissistic mothers are known to have a "golden child" and one or more "scapegoats". Mom told me an incident that took place while I was a baby. She had tried to rock me to sleep one mid-afternoon, but I had continued to cry. Her arms too tired for the task, she had made a hammock between two doorposts, and placed me in it. After a while, fed up with my ongoing screams, she gave the hammock a huge shove, sending me across the room. She said I landed in a tight space between the armoire and the headboard; and not a peep. As she slowly picked me up, she was relieved to see I was still breathing, and "sound asleep" - as she described. I thank God for putting me to sleep during the impact without any damage. Otherwise she could've killed me that day before Dad came home. I still don't know why she told me that story while I was nursing my first baby. And since it'll never make sense one way or the other, I don't care to question.

Mom obviously didn't have me because she was ready to love and nurture an innocent little baby into a healthy individual. She just needed a baby to blend in with her peers and wear the "mom" title. She expected me to mimic her and make her feel good. I was to feed her own image. I was simply another mirror to see herself in. In fact, as I showed signs of growing up into an entirely different person than she was, an independent and intelligent young lady, she felt betrayed. She was always dismissive about my successes or happy days; because if it was about me, it wasn't about her.

Jirayr was the golden child. He was the best in everything. He could do no wrong. His mistakes were glossed over and ignored. He too served a purpose; but it was different from mine. In the Middle Eastern cultures, giving birth to a boy meant earning status unlike any other. It was the ultimate validation of a woman's ego. So we were each assigned a part to play; except Jirayr's was a noble one. I remember trying to tell him a few things I had been suspecting about our mother. He didn't know where I was going with it. He was too young to understand. He looked perplexed. Only then did I realize that he hadn't endured any of my hurts and disappointments.

I had no right to taint his innocence with darkness and take away something dear to his heart. So I decided to hold everything in. Instead, I would see to it that he was never burdened with unnecessary guilt or shame. I was already the scapegoat of the family. Adding a few extra blames wouldn't have killed me.

I entered a life of torture the day my feet were tied and I couldn't escape. It was my lunch I was staring at. I didn't like it. Mom wanted me to finish what was on my plate. I had obeyed many times before; but this particular concoction was gross. It made me gag. I couldn't go through with it. So I decided to rebel. I was about four years old at the time. I remember because it gave me deep scars. Mom tied my feet to the leg of the table. She brought in my cousins and my friends to watch my humiliation. She wasn't going to untie me until I ate the whole thing. This was her idea of disciplining me. She was full of cruelties. She wasn't playing around. She went for the kill. That was the day I gave in to her authority. She grabbed the reins of my life and dragged me places no child should've gone. She was aggressive with her demands; and nothing would satisfy her. If you gave an inch, she took a mile. Her needs were massive. And I was defenseless.

She must've read a book called "What Would Hitler Do?" One of our history assignments as a teenager had been about this German dictator. He had an abusive father who believed child rearing involved beating the will out of the child. Hitler had five siblings, but only one lived past childhood. It would be fair to think that what was considered "discipline" then would be called "murder" today. His poor mother was sweet and submissive. I was surprised to find out that Hitler was born on Easter Sunday - April 20, 1889 to be exact - and baptized a Catholic. It's hard to picture him as an altar boy. I was even more shocked when I learned that Hitler painted watercolor scenes of Vienna for a living; and that he had personal and business relationships with Jews, until he no longer needed them - literally. Looking into his childhood, it's easy to discern what home environments are capable of producing. That is not to say that all children from toxic parents will turn into monsters. But no child raised in a loving environment ever turns into one.

    I'm still lucky. I could've ended up with anxieties, obsessions, or other behavioral disorders. I could've resigned to numb myself through the use of drugs and alcohol. I never became an under-achiever because of my circumstances. I assessed damages by reading self-help books; and I definitely found plenty of comfort through reading the Bible. As a result, I decided not to spend a lifetime trying to mend my relationship with Mom. I moved on, even though she was interwoven into the fabric of my being and she affected everything about my future. My journey away from her wasn't easy. I was emotionally handicapped. Limping and falling were familiar patterns of my life; but they never kept me from walking past my obstacles. I kept moving forward, one baby-step at a time.

    Both "voice" and "self" are establish during early childhood. People who have not been given voice then, have the lifelong task of needing to be heard. Self goes under construction with unexpectedly large cost overruns in order to earn a sense of value and importance. Once mutilated by a powerful person - and no one has more power over a child than a revered parent - it is highly possible to seek another powerful person who will rescue what was once lost. Anyone with a grandiose attitude and obsessive flatteries will appear right, even if they happen to be pathological liars. So I've picked people who knew to say all the right things, and appeared to love me. I needed them to validate my existence. This is the price I paid as the daughter of a narcissistic mother.

My grandmother witnessed the killings of her entire family as a young teenager. So by the time she married a much older man and had kids of her own, she was most likely shut down to just basics. And since grandpa couldn't be the bread winner due to his age, grandma went on auto-pilot and juggled many roles. Expressing love or nurturing were out of question. She was too worried about how to feed and clothe her family. Being next to the youngest, Mom must've felt like a nuisance. She wasn't old enough to contribute towards the household expenses like the rest of her siblings. And she wasn't the youngest and the most adorable any more. So her hunger to be noticed turned into an obsession she couldn't resist. By the time she had her own family, she was determined to be the screenwriter. Neither Dad nor I could've made up for what was missing in her life. Therefore, we each had to play a part designated by her manipulations.

Jirayr somehow missed her follies. By the time he was born, Mom was a lot calmer. But that's also when Dad decided to have his emotional breakdown. He left Mom for another woman. I was seven. If there had been a contest to describe "hell", I would've won the first prize. Mom was the devil. She was red hot with fury. She had horns. Her tongue was the pitchfork. She did everything in her power to find this witch, and teach her a lesson. And her lesson was:

I was to go to her house and tell this woman to leave my daddy alone!

    I was petrified. I already knew what it was like to feel unloved and unimportant until then. Mom had done a superb job reflecting her own childhood sceneries on me. And I had accepted them. But that day, I felt hated. I felt cursed. I literally thought evil beings were entering my body, eating away every fiber, every cell, until I was completely gone. I was dying on the inside. In fact, all good died that day. I stood in that corner and watched that woman's apartment, with tears running down my cheeks. Mom had taken me there. She stood by me and instructed me not to be a coward. She ordered me to go in and fight for my daddy. I was afraid out of my mind. I was afraid of Mom. I was afraid of this woman. And I was afraid of the entire situation. I cried uncontrollably. If only someone would put an end to this brutal nightmare, or take me out.

    I really wanted to die. It wasn't until I started hyperventilating that Mom finally realized her plan wasn't working out. Things started getting dark and blurry. I must've been about to lose consciousness when she decided to grab me by the wrist and dragged me home, screaming "... You'll never amount to anything... It's because of you that your daddy won't be coming home... Such a loser you are..." I believed every one of those words; because I felt them. I was given a chance to do something incredibly important and paint a smile on her face. And I hated myself for not being able to go through with it.

    Life was awful after that. Mom treated me as if I didn't exist. I had become the identified patient. All of the ills of the family were projected unto me; and I often paid out those ills. She started plotting ways to win Dad back. I really didn't want him to come back. If only I could go with him! But that didn't happen. Dad ended up coming home and spent a lifetime listening to Mom's distasteful reminders about the affair. She disciplined and controlled him with it. Unpleasant comments and occasional insults gave her the superiority she needed to tighten the reins.

Her abusive behavior became intolerable until one day I decided to tell her she was wrong for what she did to me that day. She was startled. She couldn't believe I remembered it, since I had never brought it up before. I was forty-two. I had kept quiet for thirty-five years. I thought it was time to remind her of something equally as shameful, since she had been digging at Dad for more than three decades. And immediately after her initial shock wore off she started screaming at me, "... You just made that up...You'll never change... You've always been a trouble maker... " I kept smiling through her demeaning comments. They no longer had any effect on me. I told her kindly "You are forgiven"; and in return, she had to forgive Dad. Her evil deed had been safe with me for a long time; but not because she had deserved the secrecy. It is called "grace". Like I said before, reading the Bible had given me many advantages over her mental and emotional inadequacies. This has been my only solemn declaration of war against Mom. I knew something awful about her no one else knew. And I used it for leverage. I'd do anything to set Dad free. Mom's lowered brows over her brooding eyes were a sign that I'd won. She never spoke of the affair after that. And she never will.

We may never know when we'll reach a level of fearlessness someday. Heroism is not about transcending others at whatever cost; it's about serving others at whatever cost.   One's liberty always come with a price.   And someone has to be brave enough to face all possible damage; yet rise above it.   Dad's actions and love shaped who I became.   Was I fortunate enough to do something for him in return?   I certainly hope so!   It felt like a part of me was completely healed that day.   I had finally stood up, looked her straight in the eyes and said, "No more!"   And Mom got the message loud and clear. My transformation wasn't overnight.   It was subtle.   One of the self-help books I'd read in the past was called "Return To Love" by Marianne Williamson.   This book had taken my breath away.   It had told me about God's love for me.   It had explained how valuable I was to Him.   It had assured me that God was pleased with me; and that He had no reason to punish me.   It had even convinced me that God saw potential in me; because He had placed it there Himself!

Once I understood my worth, I became very sad for my mother.   She obviously never knew what God thought of her.   She couldn't have; if she had to belittle others in order to feel good about herself.   Her need to dominate everything ended up controlling her. It robbed her of the pleasure of loving her own child.   It cost her great measures of love and happiness she never knew she had at her fingertips.   She fell prey to her own weapon.   She'll never know how I would've wanted to worship her.   She never knew how much Dad cherished her.   He loved her with all of her flaws.   He worshipped the ground she walked on.   He did everything for her.   She didn't even have to ask.   In fact, she ordered him around quite often.

Dad didn't mind.   He was like Popeye the Sailor Man around his love interest Olive Oyl.   She was prone to get angry over the tiniest things and challenged Popeye's near-saintly perseverance in overcoming any obstacle to please her.   This cartoon character was mainly known with his pipe and his spinach.   His pipe served as a cutting torch, a jet engine, a propeller, a periscope, and was known for its famous toot.   Spinach gave him strength and endurance.   With it, Popeye was capable of coming up with solutions to all problems.   I'd like to say Dad's pipe was his integrity.   He relied on it to persevere, to overcome, and to conquer every emotional trauma Mom dragged him into.   And his spinach was us, Jirayr and I, who gave him the strength to keep it together, to stand tall, and to laugh away the disappointments of life.   Mom could've chosen to have us in order to hold on to her marriage.   She was not mother material.   Yet she never knew we ended up being Dad's only reason for fortitude and stamina throughout her plots.

   Emotional abuse is an attempt to destroy the will, needs, desires, or perceptions of someone who happens to be a part of your life.   It's often continuous and omnipresent.   Name calling, obscenities, belittling, downgrading, and shaming are just as bad as physical abuse; if not worse.   Yet physical abuse is usually intermittent, and its results heal.   Emotional and mental scars remain buried for years.   They give birth to all sorts of vulnerabilities and character flaws.   Often, they're expressed in the form of rage and anger.   And sometimes they take shape as numbness of emotions.   And because abusers blame their victims, there's always that guilt factor.   Shame tags along.   It could be an alcoholic father.   It could be a druggy relative.   Innocence is marred.   You shut down.   You hide behind a smile while wiping away the invisible tears of your soul.   You hide from friends and relatives who might pity you.   You even hide your pain from yourself, because no burden is heavier to bear than the burden of a false idea.   It takes time and effort to identify emotional and mental abuse.

   I was unaware of my situation for a long time.   I knew my mother had a problem with me.   And since she appeared to be a highly functioning individual, it would've been fair to think that I was the problem.   I walked on egg shells.   I took the blame just so there would be no arguments.   I apologized for things I couldn't have been responsible for.   Keeping her calm became my duty.   I didn't complain.   I didn't dare have an opinion.   I went along with her ideas even if I didn't agree.   I lost my voice.   I became her caregiver in the most twisted way; because she lacked the fundamentals of mothering. There was a role reversal early on.   I grew up quick.   To this day, sometimes Mom will start a sentence with, "you're so much like me..." or "I used to be just like you...", and I cringe.   Not only do I not see any resemblance; but I pray there wouldn't be any found.   I'd rather die than hurt my children.   Mom was still a role model though; I did everything in my power not to be like her.

   If we are born with the inability to comprehend right from wrong, then it would be fair to believe we're innocent at birth.   The Bible says, "Man is the image and glory of God" according to 1 Corinthians 11: 7.   There are many parallel verses that enforce this description.   Therefore, we must all be dressed in purity as we land safely into our parents' arms.   We remain innocent until our sinful nature is awakened by the mini corruptions of those from whom we are supposed to learn.   Wouldn't it be lovely if our innocence taught them how delightful and simple life is meant to be?   And what happens when that most precious virtue is taken away prematurely? It is made of all the raw materials necessary for who we are when we're born, rather than who we become at the end. It possesses the right ingredients to land us on the path we're meant to journey on. We already know innocence cannot be restored. What's there to enjoy when you're too busy changing that little person, and substituting all the good attributes within? How do you propose its trustfulness and joyfulness be reinstated? And what kind of pleasure can there be when those beautiful eyes no longer light up when they see you nearing them?

My mother's approach was critical in determining the kind of relationship she and I would end up having. Nothing is sadder than the kind of ignorance that overlooks a child's sweet disposition; and thus believes punishment is a must to set her straight. She either broke me so well that I wouldn't dare rebel against her escalating tactics; or by the grace of God, I learned humility and submission early enough to be more pliable against her vicious attacks. Either way my fate remained under construction, without harming those under my care, until I would be given an opportunity to overcome those damages. I saw to it that my children would never taste the bitterness my mother decided to leave behind. Her mental and emotional disorders weren't going to be passed down to the next generation. I, as a parent, was given that privilege not once, but twice. I made sure my kids didn't become like me.

Divorcing my mother was the number one step towards my recovery. I had a hard time accepting the fact that I was never loved by my mother; because I wasn't taught to deal with feelings. I made an effort to separate myself from my mother physically as well as psychologically; and decided which direction I should go. There were only two choices: I could either follow in her footsteps or refuse to.

Education was also a great weapon against my tormented childhood. It provided me resources and answers I needed in order to get to the root of the problem. Life's negative patterns often stem from an unhealthy upbringing. And it takes a tremendous amount of courage to overcome the ill-effects of trauma endured at a young age.

Life is simple after three disasters. I'm very selective these days. Dating and having a good time is fun. But it's not because I need to be validated by someone. I like who I am. I'm totally content. Being stuck with the wrong person is the worst kind of loneliness. I've already done that enough times. So I'd rather feel lonely occasionally. I hang out with friends. I look after my business. I visit my kids every now and then. I go on vacations. I have a good life. I've chased away insecurities. I celebrate the fact that I didn't pass down the virus. It was eradicated through me. Mom's problems stopped polluting innocent lives.

I guess because of the amount of pain I endured growing up, I have a lot of compassion for people who are experiencing disappointments. I can easily cry with them. I feel their pain. Most of the time they just need someone to hear them out. They're not ready for suggestions. They just need to empty out their accumulated emotions. Some can't believe that another person would actually make time to listen. They're like a pouch of popcorn in the microwave. At the beginning the tiny kernels sound like they're racing with one another. They pop back to back for a good three minutes or so. Then the excitement dies down. You may hear a few pops with two or three second intervals. And then you push the stop button and get the bag out. People with accumulated emotions, once they know they can trust you with their secret, can't speak fast enough. But thirty or forty-five minutes later, they start slowing down. They even start repeating a few of their previous sentences.

I wait until they stop popping. Only then are they ready to hear what I might have to share with them. I tell them about a certain experience of mine. I want them to see that I've walked in their shoes. I also tell them what made a huge difference in my case: a sincere belief in God's love for me and an ongoing intimate relationship with Him. After all, once I received God's seal of approval, Mom's approval didn't matter. If God needed to protect me from my own mother, why would I sulk over the fact that Mom never loved me? It's her loss; not mine. She'll never taste what I've received through loving my two children unconditionally. And she'll never grow old with the kind of memorable moments I get to have with my kids.

I often wondered why it wasn't possible for Mom to raise me with unconditional love. Now I know the answer. The source of such love is God, without whom we cannot possess anything good and valuable. Mom told me about her own dad who was an older gentleman, more like a grandfather figure in the house. She remembers him sitting on the sofa, all day long, reading the Bible. Every now and then he would suggest, "Come, sit with me a while, and read a little..." Mom's response was, "You're doing a fine job. Keep it up..." How sad to know that Mom too had a dad who wanted to give her something of value, but her stubbornness got in the way. She never got to know God's love for her. If she did, she wouldn't have grown up with confidence issues. She wouldn't have needed to subtract every bit of self-worth out of her own daughter in order to feel superior. Why would anyone compete with a child?

Dad passed away nine years ago. His battle against pancreatic cancer lasted five weeks. He didn't suffer long. He didn't endure unnecessary procedures. Mom and I were able to be in one accord. There was no fighting. For the first time ever we went along with each other's suggestions. During the funeral, she looked up with tears streaming down both cheeks and said, "I'm so sorry!" I asked, "Why?" She explained, "I never allowed you to cry. I now know it was wrong. I'm sorry..." I had forgotten that one until she brought it up.

Mom has been under my care ever since. I visit her regularly. I look after her and provide her needs. I can't say that I love her as my "mother" because she never was that for me. But I can honestly say that it's possible to love her as a person who happens to have an incurable disease. It's easier to love people we admire. But it takes sacrifice to extend our love to those who don't deserve it. And, sacrifice is a form of discipline that brings on spiritual growth and contentment. I want to attain all that. I want the rest of my life to be the best. How I fulfill my responsibilities towards Mom these days shouldn't be based on how she handled hers in the past. If I choose to step into that trap now, I would be restored back to my previous position as an extension of her. And going back wouldn't be fair to that little girl whose feet were tied to a table so she would eat her food. I fought hard for her freedom.

CHAPTER 3.   JIRAYR

As the sunny evening unfolds, I thank God for the ability to observe details of which many aren't aware.   They're either too involved in their circumstances or don't know to appreciate the simple yet majestic things of life.   I watch a celestial double rainbow grace the sky, as the backside of the storm scurries to another occasion. The luminous display is breathtakingly beautiful.   It's poetry.   It speaks of new beginnings.   I also notice the suspended droplets until they grow heavy enough to fall into minuscule spatters.   They are a part of the final movement of a concerto, composed to dismiss you with the greatest satisfaction possible.   Their attendance is equally as important during this epic black-tie affair.   I have a heightened sensitivity to the promises of life.   It's there because of hope and optimism Dad planted years ago.

I must pursue my dreams; even if it means I'll have to join my creative inner self permanently.   Many of my childhood disappointments found happy endings, not because I asked others for help.   But because I waited patiently for things to heal and birth happier results.   My position in life was unclear at the beginning.   I knew Dad loved me; but Mom's mixed signals confused me all the time.   I didn't know my place.   Nor did I recognize what I was good for.   Yet all that perplexity faded away one day with the arrival of a huge gift from above.

Becoming a sister injected me with a sense of responsibility I still carry around like a trophy.   It gave me a purpose.   It added color to my dull existence.   Someone would need me after all!   I would stop being a shadow. And that feeling built me up. Jirayr's little presence was huge for me. It became my strength. As he cried less and less, he became my playmate. I included him in my imaginary adventures. He looked up to me for his next assignments. He never refused to cooperate. To him, I was not a nuisance. He enjoyed my company. His sweet nature made up for everything else. He was easy to love. His love didn't need to be earned!

Often we laid on the floor, looking out the window, trying to glimpse an airplane in the clouds. And as soon as we detected one, we made up unlimited stories. Through the eyes of our imagination, we were on that plane, going to Paris to visit the art galleries of the Louvre. Then we went up the Eiffel Tower and had a panoramic view of the city. We then talked about cruising through the canals of Venice in a gondola and eating gelato. The famous composers of Austria whose names we couldn't pronounce invited us to the symphony and we dressed up quickly to look impressive. Jirayr went along with every idea. He laughed and carried on with his little words. He acted his part very well. He even sang on stage occasionally as a performer, holding the extension cord as a microphone, while I applauded with excitement. He took a bow and acknowledged my praise with a huge grin. His eyes lit up with happiness. He was my happiness!

Jirayr was a beautiful child. He had unique features. His curly hair was dirty blonde. His eyes were blue. His skin was peachy like Mom's; unlike the olive complexion Dad and I shared. I loved him from the moment I laid eyes on him. I wanted to be around him all the time. He was a breath of fresh air in my rigid world of discipline.

The innocence in his eyes was remarkable. It was soothing to me. His birth calmed the tensions of our family. And my heart double thumped when I saw the way he looked at me. I saw no judgment or prejudice. Was it possible for this little parson to love me the way I loved him? The thought thrilled me. My unbending will to survive wasn't challenged by him. I could be me around him.

He cried often though. I kept hearing the term "colicky". I guess it had something to do with his tummy. I kept praying that he would stop hurting. I felt bad for him. I wanted to burp him as I had seen others do, and make him feel better. And I also wanted to make Mom like me. I was only seven; even though she treated me like an adult. The conjunction of Jirayr's birth and my older cousin Selvi's adoption into our family placed me at the bottom of Mom's list of priorities. He was the long awaited baby boy through whom she received a place of honor. And my sweet cousin, being ejected from her own dysfunctional background, became Mom's instant companion and a built-in babysitter. From that moment on, my presence was noticed only if and when I got in some kind of trouble.

A good portion of Mom's unhappiness disappeared by the birth of a son. And that upgraded me. It lessened the verbal and emotional abuse. It also made me completely invisible. I longed to be validated. Would Mom notice if I disappeared? Would she even care? I found those answers one day as I let go of her hand during our walk back from school. She merged into the crowded streets of Istanbul, not realizing I wasn't with her. I'll never forget the crowd forming around me and the police officer asking me all sorts of questions. Lost had a different meaning that day. One old man insisted he knew my family; and that he would take me to them. I'd never seen him before. I choked with fear. Tears streamed down my face; and my heart sobbed. I don't know which I grieved more. Was it the fact that I was lost, or the fact that Mom hadn't noticed I was gone?

    I excelled at being "out of sight". And now I was "out of mind." I don't know what frightened me the most. Was I scared of being alone in that crowd, since I was a nobody to everyone around? Or was it the fact that I was a nobody in my own mother's eyes? I think the latter damaged me the most. Mom and I walked home every day after school. I should've known the way. When she disappeared; I was devastated. Total strangers realized I was lost. They gathered around to help. Mom was gone. She never looked back. She never told me she loved me.

    Suddenly, she appeared and parted the crowd. She grabbed me by the wrist, and whisked me away from the police officer and the rest. She walked fast. I had to run to keep up with her. She was furious. I interrupted her busy schedule. Hugging or comforting me never crossed her mind. "You shouldn't have let go my hand! That was dumb!" I kept hearing. When we got home, I went straight to my room and stayed there. I cried and cried. It was time to bury an identity that was never to be mine. I was not a daughter; I was an inconvenience. And fears of never being able to see Dad overwhelmed me. No grief could compete with that. I still don't know if Mom didn't notice I was missing or she opted to wait a while in order to teach me a lesson. I never questioned her. I was afraid to. I really don't care to know the answer. It won't fix anything!

I used to spend hours in my bedroom. It was my cocoon; my safe place. Through my vivid imagination, I dressed in identities such as a queen or a princess. I envisioned my servants rushing in as I rang the bell and bringing me breakfast in bed. They prepared my bath and washed my hair. They attended to my appearance. They laid out my gowns and assisted me in dressing. I had a personal stylist who fixed my hair and makeup. I was covered in the most expensive jewels. I was confident and I had power. And on the days I didn't feel like ruling and judging, I decided to become a professor or a renowned scientist. I longed to feed young minds and help them towards better and brighter futures. I wanted to change the world. I would use either power or knowledge. My dreams of becoming a beacon for many still urge me to do good works. I yearn to make a difference. My greatest desire is to sprinkle the world with fairness and kindness.

When I have moments of "woe is me," I fight back. That's my way of honoring Dad's sacrifices. I'll do that for the rest of my life. I admire my brother Jirayr for that reason. He is more like Dad. I work hard to gain the qualities those two possess naturally. They both saw humor in everything. Darkness didn't stand a chance with them. They laughed their mistakes away, and smiled through life's hiccups; while I barely forced a smile. I concealed my sadness and hopelessness. I wore a mask to give me strength. My facial muscles were challenged if I laughed out loud. I wasn't *shy* as everyone referred to me. I was overlooked. Since bad moods and acting up were not allowed, I held on to Dad to ride the rougher waves. I had recurring dreams of falling into an abyss. Nobody recognized the signs. My good dreams were about a pink donkey. His entire body was pink. I ran around with him all night long, and woke up happy. Every time Dad tucked me in, he whispered, "Don't forget to say *Hi* to your pink donkey for me."

Eeyore from Winnie the Pooh was my favorite cartoon character. First of all, because he was a donkey. I knew all about donkeys. I saw them during our summers on the island. They carried heavy loads for the local merchants or the nearby construction sites. I felt sorry for them. It seemed they never got to rest. And Eeyore was a sad one. He was old and grey, and extremely depressed. His long detachable tail with a pink bow at the end was what made me care for him. I could relate to him. I too carried burdens too heavy for my age. I believed nothing could help me, because I didn't know what needed to be fixed; nor did I know who could fix me. Though I worked hard and became a high achiever in school, deep inside I felt alone and inadequate. Eeyore's pink bow symbolized all the pretty dreams I had of a "happy family." I didn't like it when he lost his tail. It was as though I was doomed forever.

Looking back, I see that I exaggerated. Forever was a big word for a seven-year-old. But feeling unimportant is like forever for anyone. I was too young to know how my views would change some day. My studies eventually led me to the Word of God, where I learned that I'm loved, regardless of my flaws. That didn't give me an automatic immunity against depression; but it was a cane to grab for stability. I now believe there's no such thing as a perfect family, because there's no such thing as a perfect person. The ideal family is the unity of two different people with the same values and an unwavering determination to stay true to their initial vows. Everyone is guaranteed unexpected situations. Those could be physical, emotional, or financial. Life isn't meant to be a smooth sail. Great testimonies result from challenging circumstances. The outcome is different for each of us. We either handle them; or they handle us!

It wasn't easy for our parents to send Jirayr and me to private schools. Though they tried to keep us in safe environments, they also exposed us to many surprising new things we didn't know existed. I saw how much more other families had in comparison to mine. If I asked for something, I was considered ungrateful at my house. Mom always said, "If you ask, you will *not* get!" It was hard to observe the material possessions and spendable income my friends had. I wished I could be like them. I wanted pretty things. If they weren't passed down through my family; then I was going to achieve these things someday. I would be successful.

I wanted store-bought clothes instead of those my aunt sewed for me. Having less than others must've truly affected me because most of my imaginary games with Jirayr involved a lavish lifestyle; such as flying to Paris for dinner; or listening to a symphony in Austria; or visiting the museums of Russia! We dreamed of being wealthy. We would own a limousine. Dad would work for us as our driver; while Mom would satisfy our taste buds as our personal chef. Certain foods like liver, okra, or spinach wouldn't be allowed! Choice meals and pastries would be her ongoing assignment. And we would have our favorite desserts. The only thing we had a hard time figuring out was if we would pay wages. Mom and Dad were going to live in an efficiency built next to our huge mansion. At some point, we agreed to give them something; because we felt "bad" for them.

I guess we could've divorced them all together; but we knew their unintentional abuse was a result of their tenuous relationship. Their inability to achieve balance in the family went out of control until one became extremely passive to survive the weaknesses of the other. While we were still children, we silently decided not to punish our parents forever; but to establish boundaries to lessen the toxicity of their effect on us.   Many people who grow up in abusive households receive the same suggestion from their therapist.   I'm amazed by the level of love and compassion Jirayr and I managed to extend to those who didn't have it together; while the outside world noticed nothing out of the ordinary.

Dad occupied himself in his spare time with writing.   What appeared to be a hobby at the time was in fact his refuge for sanity. He penned humor-filled thoughts and comments.   He wrote because he didn't have anyone with whom he could share a conversation. Conferring with Mom brought on conflict, because she wanted to argue.   So he never expressed himself honestly.   Whatever we learned from Dad, without attracting Mom's criticism, we learned by observing him.   Though we never read any of his compositions, Jirayr and I inherited Dad's approach to life.   That's an amazing miracle!   If Dad's sound teachings made it past Mom's aggressive and boisterous lectures, then they must have broken through with a great invisible force.   Those things were passed down and planted in us, without Mom's awareness.   I thank God for it!

Dad found contentment in his family life.   He was at his destination.   He never needed to know what else he could have.   He was fulfilled.   His purpose was to provide well and to protect well.

He was a wonderful father. And Jirayr followed in Dad's footsteps. He too is an excellent father. He would die for any of his three kids. Dad's five grandchildren, including my two, display all the good qualities we found in him. So what happened to all the flawed behaviors we were exposed to as kids? Yelling and screaming; argumentative and aggressive outbursts; jealousy and false pride! The same thing that happened to tyrants and murderers throughout history! They each caused grief for a while; but at the end, they all fell. Evil is the absence of good; it has no power on its own. The source of good will always triumph over evil.

Most people reward "good" and they do not tolerate "bad". When someone lies to us, we stop trusting that person. Therefore, we stop associating with him. At the end, the natural consequences catch up, and bad people reap what they've sown. We don't need to wish it on them. Everyone makes a better decision if they listen to their conscience. It's there to help us shift in the right direction. But if we're easily swayed by others' opinions that contradict our instincts - in other words if we're people pleasers - then we quiet that inner voice; so we can be a part of a larger crowd. But the consequences find us, wherever we are, sooner or later.

The only problem with that inner voice is that we don't tolerate being told what *not* to do. Yet we are designed to be moral beings. And our conscience reminds us when we go off and violate a moral code. The minute we dismiss the warning sounds, we justify and rationalize our behavior. A good rule of thumb is, "when we look for plausible reasons to do something, we already know it's wrong." Everyone has a duty to constantly shape, monitor, and maintain their conscience by simply yielding to it. And the more we practice it, the more accurate become its promptings.

No one should rely on appearances. I'm considered an introvert. I'm a thinker and an observer. I have much to say, yet I prefer silence. And the more I learn, the less I know! To me, life is a series of lessons. I don't want to waste a minute of it trying to impress others. I don't do pretense. I find substance is highly valuable. I look at things and try to figure out how they relate to me. What can I learn from them? I want to better myself. And I know I'm not done. I have much to accomplish. Flashing ideas to look and sound important doesn't cross my mind. I find it difficult to function in a world where many people are pretenders. They receive praise while ignoring rules and regulations that should apply to them as well. Yet "Don't get caught" is the only rule they obey. I need to understand! If there is a rule, there must be a reason for it! I am a cynic in a world of fakes.

We either pay the price of discipline, or the price of regret. These tenets apply to career, health, family and finance issues. If we don't practice self-control and integrity, we'll accumulate misdeeds that will haunt us to the end. Whether we use arrogance or ignorance as an excuse; neither keeps us from facing serious repercussions. We must pay attention to our quiet, persistent inner voice. It urges us to change something or learn from a previous mistake so we won't repeat it. There have been many evildoers throughout history, especially those in power, who tormented and killed millions of people. We have that kind of power with our words. We can kill someone's spirit or self-worth with one sentence.

The greatest compliment that came from my mother was when I was in my early fifties. She said, "I learned what parenting is all about through watching you with your children." It didn't come in the form of an apology; but it *was* the apology. That was Mom's first time admitting she failed. It also showed me that I had shed some light on the darkness she had been living in. Not helping her would've been immoral. And even though Dad was gone, she was finally appreciating his gentle ways that shaped the kind of parent I am today. He never got to hear any such statement, but he didn't need it. He was already solid.

Unfortunately, Dad's sense of contentment wasn't passed down. Both Jirayr and I became aggressive in our work. Partly because that's all we had dreamed of. We were going to be wealthy. Owning homes and fancy vehicles were all we talked about as kids. I was the culprit. Traveling for fun and offering the best to our children was exactly what we wanted out of life. To us, a fulfilled lifestyle meant success. And success brought in the wealth. All limitations are extinguished with it! But seriously, if you leave an entire lifestyle behind and start over, you tend to go on auto-pilot, aiming to catch up with things you once had. That's the most natural reaction. The refugee diffidence stalks all of us. It's in our blood.

Dad helped me open a beauty shop. He built the stations, the cabinets, and the retail shelves. I hired subcontractors for the plumbing and the electrical work. It was all done in less than a month. I've thanked God for the gift of owning my own business for over twenty-five years. I still love every moment of it. Jirayr started in the jewelry field as an apprentice at age seventeen. He was very good at it. Dad helped him establish a business also. Jirayr's upbeat personality opened many doors as business liaisons. He hired people so he could travel and bring in more orders. He became highly successful.

      A good portion of our childhood travel plans didn't come true; but they served as a foundation for a healthy outlook. They helped us develop a positive mindset to overcome life's liabilities. They also programmed our imagination to tap into the unthinkable. Who knew Jirayr would end up as a great businessman some day? That he would go to the Far East on business trips? That he and his family would take vacations throughout the Caribbean islands? And that I would also take my two children on vacations, and observe different cultures? Our resourcefulness was what made the difference. And for that, we both owe Dad a lot.

      My brother and I have many things in common. We laugh over silly things. His jokes are funnier. We work hard. Though we both prefer to have the best, we're always thankful for the smallest results. We're encouragers. We dislike dark conversation. We'll go any distance to avoid complainers. And we love dancing, parties, and entertainment. We enjoy dressing up. Jirayr looks great even in casuals. Mine is rather a necessity. I either emphasize or counteract the mood I'm in. Some days I wear something special and put on heavier makeup to help me feel good. Often I try on several different looks before I choose one. I don't do it to impress others. I simply enjoy looking good. And since I don't have to share my space with anyone else, tidying it up waits for the weekend. Or until I can no longer find what I'm looking for.

Jirayr and I have failed relationships in our pasts; partly because we were sheltered.   We were told to stay away from "bad" people; but we weren't taught how to protect ourselves against them. Many restrictions; but never intelligent explanations!   So we were afraid to reveal our mistakes.   Life was without guidance, a ritual of trial and error.   We had bad results our parents didn't hear about; yet we never hid them from our children.   We wanted them to learn that failure was just as human as success.   We didn't waste time questioning the "Why me?"   We simply focused on what we could learn from mistakes, or what was the best approach not to have the same result.   We don't view life's struggles as daunting obstacles to our happiness.   They are the keys to our happiness; because learning is a part of happiness.   Being stagnant stunts our potential for happiness.   We didn't give up.   We focused on our strengths.   To this day, we still encourage one another.   Giving up is not an option.

Einstein, considered by many the smartest man of the last century, didn't begin to speak until he was 4 years old.   I'm sure there were people concerned about his developmental progress.   Isaac Newton, scientist and discoverer of gravity, did very poorly in grade school, and was considered by his teachers to have an "unpromising future."   As we know well, the critics failed.   Beethoven, one of history's greatest musical composers, was told by his music teacher that "he is hopeless."   And Thomas Edison was told by his teacher that he was "too stupid" to learn!   What kind of teacher does that to a child?   Walt Disney was fired by his newspaper editor because "he lacked imagination."   If only she knew how impaired her own imagination was at the time!   Our predictions are flawed because we don't know the potential within.   Looking at a tiny piece of a jigsaw puzzle will not help us see what we are looking at until we see it within the big picture. Likewise, when we're able to see the bigger picture, then the little troubles of the past start making sense.

Sometimes things don't go the way we want. And sometimes we fail because of something outside of our control. We may lose a job due to downsizing. We may lose our crops due to unfavorable weather conditions. We may even lose someone we hoped to share a lifetime with. But those setbacks don't determine how our lives will turn out. A grim forecast of the future stems from confusion and unbelief. We either don't believe grief can be overcome; or we don't care to overcome it. Because we possess every drop of strength to walk against the grain, we must place one foot in front of the other, and accomplish what appears to be impossible. There is always a port after a rough sea. Not everything turns out as expected; but even mistakes often bring laughter in our later years.

Lee Marvin, Clint Eastwood, and Jean Seberg starred in an old musical called "Paint Your Wagon". They were not singers by the stretch of anybody's imagination; but their graceful good humor disarmed the criticism the movie deserved. It was about a rustic mining camp, No Name City, during the height of the California gold rush. The chaos created by bad choices came out in boisterous processions and town meetings. People spouted peculiar psychological implications until the entire town was destroyed; and everyone had to start over elsewhere. In some ways, this movie's weaknesses were its virtues. It was cheerful. It was entertaining. Yet nothing about the script made sense. Sometimes, we try too hard to understand our blunders. Not everything in life will make sense.   We must learn to laugh at ourselves.

Having a sense of humor about things makes life easier.   The ability to laugh at ourselves comes from good humor and an optimistic personality.   It also shows that we can forgive ourselves.   Stressing over the controllable and the uncontrollable, and worrying about every wrongdoing harms us.   We are irritated, aggravated, and annoyed at the slightest inconvenience.   Overthinking reduces us to a small drop from a heavy and burdened heart.   Our time on earth is valuable.   Why theorize and postulate? Just jump in with both feet!   Why give way to ulcers and panic attacks when we already know "what will be, will be" at the end?   That doesn't mean we should roll over and play dead because our efforts don't count.   It simply means our fears and worries will always sabotage the better results time and patience will produce.   God designed everything to bring forth good fruit.   All things have a way of working out.   It's like going white water rafting and following the guide's instructions during the entire trip, while your heart pumps extra blood to match the survival mode you are in.   It's a surprise at the end when you find out the guide didn't need any help!   It was part of the adventure!

Have you ever watched the birth of a giraffe?   The first thing to emerge is the baby giraffe's front hooves and head.   A few minutes later, its entire body falls about ten feet, landing on its back.   Within seconds he rolls to an upright position with his legs tucked under his body.   The mother giraffe positions herself directly over her calf and kicks her baby hard enough to send it sprawling head over heels!   When it doesn't get up, this violent process is repeated, over and over again, until the baby calf stands for the first time on its wobbly legs.

Then the mother kicks it off its feet again, because she wants it to remember how it got up. This tutorial is vital for its survival. In the wild, baby giraffes must be able to get up as quickly as possible to stay with the herd, lest it'll be lions' or hyenas' dinner. Animals don't have the intellect we possess. Yet their instincts are right on the money. They know exactly what to do.

In fact, there are parenting skills in the animal kingdom that put humans to shame. On average, an octopus lays between 50,000 and 200,000 eggs while giving birth. To ensure their survival, she'll separate the eggs into groups based upon factors like size, shape and likeliness of survival. She then dedicates the next two months of her life protecting them from predators and ensuring they get enough oxygen by pushing water currents towards the eggs. Because she is so busy keeping them alive, she doesn't have time to feed herself. So she often ends up passing away shortly after they hatch.

God programmed all of His creatures, including us, to act and react based on better and more profitable results. We may think failure holds us back and hinders our progress. Actually, it helps us spring forth to accomplish more. A failure in the past doesn't make us a failure. It's there to learn from and do better the next time. We must roll with the punches, grow from the obstacles, and get over the petty and insignificant details to enjoy success. Having achievements and overcoming challenges is what defines success for some. And others might measure it with the amassing of properties and goods. I believe emotional success outweighs all other, giving us the freedom to enjoy the rest.

Jirayr and I both believed being financially comfortable was an evidence of success and happiness. We learned our lesson through trial and error. The Bible says the love of money is the root of all evil. The love of money is a decision or desire to pursue wealth for personal consumption or luxury. Its purpose stems from a lack of contentment. The Bible portrays it as, "The lust of the flesh, the lust of the eye, and the boastful pride of life." Every one of those temptations come from a lack of contentment. Its emotional claws tug at our insides. We long for its comforting appeal. It's either a deliberate choice, or a strong longing to be rich. That focus puts us on the Wrong Path! We see so many celebrities who feel entitled to do whatever they please, without considering the consequences.

There is nothing wrong with wanting wealth and status, and working hard to achieve both. But a huge yearning for them presents a problem concerning our self-esteem. If it takes so much effort to keep us happy and content, we might not be happy and content with who we are. Otherwise we wouldn't be so concerned with outward elements. Feeling good about ourselves is very important to a contented life. If we value ourselves unconditionally, including our strengths and our weaknesses, then we free ourselves from external opinions. Any obsession is always followed by a hard and a painful lesson. Ours was called "bankruptcy." Jirayr and I found ourselves dealing with it just about the same time. I faced mine early on. His followed several years later. Most people who have money want more; just like we did. It's never enough! Money may highlight priorities; but it doesn't buy the most important things such as love, health, and spiritual maturity.

The love of money is at the root of many problems. It lives inside of us and nourishes us with all kinds of lies. It also determines our fruit. Love of money is just like a weed. It sends down a taproot that can support an invasive tree! If left alone, it will take over the yard! It will suck all the water and nutrients from the beautiful, fruit-full trees. We must fight such invasion. If we only yank the invaders out and don't destroy all of the roots, they'll spring up in another spot; just like the love of money will spring up in other parts of our lives until it takes over and destroys us. It's deceptive. It feeds us a false sense of contentment that only money can buy. It never lasts and it never brings happiness. I read somewhere that money will buy a bed but not sleep; books but not brains; food but not appetite; finery but not beauty; a house but not a home; medicine but not health; luxuries but not culture; amusements but not happiness; religion but not salvation; a passport to everywhere but heaven. That is true wisdom!

There is an intimate connection between who we are and how we handle our finances. It displays the wisdom we apply to decisions. Money is not the problem; it's our attitude towards it that is. Money is dangerous just like loaded guns are dangerous. Both are useful in certain situations if we're careful. We need to treat them with respect and know how to use them; because they have the capacity to harm us. They can destroy us and our families.

When we are given life by The Divine Being, we are valuable to Him. Our innocence is priceless. Not only does His infinite patience take time to carve each and every one of us with unique details; but He also gives us an identity. The hidden insights and resources help fulfill His purpose for us. All of our God-given treasure is buried in the cavity of our heart. He doesn't want us to struggle. We're to be conquerors. Believe it or not, we are complete products at birth. This world can't enhance what's placed within us. If anything; it will deduct from it in a heartbeat. That's why looking in the mirror comforts me from time to time. It's as if I'm trying to get a visual of what was once mine. If only I could turn back time and reclaim some of the purity!

That place of peace and sanity is what the world tries to disturb every now and then. Jirayr and I both had our share of challenges. We were too trusting. We both gave in to aggressive partners. Their dysfunctions became ours. We both fought to stay afloat in a sea of turmoil. These days, we try to process things with reason; and try to give our feelings a much deserved rest.

Jirayr and I had one extremely passive and one extremely aggressive parent. Towards the end, there were no discussions to clear away the everyday stuff. Brushing things under the rug was the only way to find peace. I ended up feeling sorry for Mom. During the later years of their marriage, tired of the ongoing hush, she would ask Dad to say two words now and then. Dad's response irritated her even more. He would say, "one...two..." with a smile. The silence between the two was deafening. It hurt them. And It hurt us. We never spoke to them about it because we didn't want things to collapse. We found our way through hit or miss kind of judgment calls. If we happened to have a good result, Mom took credit. And if we didn't, it had to be Dad's fault. He simply smiled. We both know now someone's greatness isn't determined by wealth or success as the majority claims; but rather by what it takes to bring them down. And nothing discouraged Dad.

Success is different from one person to another. An executive can go to a coffee shop every day and pick up a pastry to go along with his cup of coffee; and think nothing of it. Yet if you're a beggar on the street corner, walking into the same shop and treating yourself to a pastry once in a blue moon is a huge success. As if such an accomplishment sprinkles magic additives to the taste; he or she savors each bite and tries to make it last. Similarly, for someone who is used to getting what they want, one small setback is intolerable; whereas a homeless person will hardly even notice it.

Failure and fault were inseparable in our household. Admitting a failure meant "we either didn't do it right", or "we didn't try hard enough". There was always something or someone to blame, instead of using encouraging words to comfort us. So we didn't share everything with our parents. Considering the infinite number of things that could've gone wrong without the proper guidance, we were still good learners. Our greatest asset was the fact that we were humble enough to admit our mistakes, without living in denial. Our hope for the best and wanting to avoid failure didn't keep us from the harsh truth. We didn't try to pull a rabbit out of a hat. The stigma of failure didn't touch us.

The ideas of success and failure are products of the society we live in. Our religion and culture train us to believe certain things. Becoming a slave to those things is the ultimate defeat and causes dependency. That leads us to compromise relationships and to give in to the demands of others.   Developing our individuality is true success!   Negative situations can make us stronger and better. Through those, we set boundaries and define new limits.   A relationship doesn't include competition.   Nor does it include power or control.   It's a harmony where equal partners deal with conflicts in fair ways.   Otherwise we haven't learned a thing from the past.

CHAPTER 4. GOD

World War II left tension between two great powers around 1947. The United States and its non-Communist allies, also known as the Western Bloc, were referred to as the First World. The Communist or the Eastern Bloc was considered the Second World. And the rest, predominantly poor, was the Third World. The impoverished countries' exceptional wealth inequality became an eye sore while they failed in health care of their population. The other two failed just as immensely by creating their own maladies in the form of discrimination due to wealth, power, and race; or by outsourcing the production of goods and services. They lost in a bigger way because they started out with so much more. Therefore "inequality" is everywhere now. Today's two terms, "developing nations" and "poor countries", is the most appropriate way to describe the world we live in.

The deterioration of social etiquette and unity within the developed nations are considered steps backward for humanity, versus the connectedness in the rest due to the common desperations. Unity is important within family members. And it's just as important within the people of a nation. Needs and concerns are highly important for "oneness". And the erosion of unity is a great challenge to overcome as we're walking towards huge mountains such as nuclear warfare and global warming. It's time to be transparent. One can't continue to hide behind his previous identity if he hasn't been living up to its definition.

This is just the physical and economical display of the world today. The spiritual decline in the developing countries is also noteworthy, since people are more single-minded and self-reliant; whereas people of the poor nations are humble and broken due to their circumstances. Desperation increases the necessity of believing in something other than "self". Those people need to cling to a power they don't possess. So the idea of God spreads like wildfire among the poor countries. And once they understand the importance of God's promises, then their physical stress about dire circumstances diminishes. People in developed countries endure far more stress because they believe they must handle it all. They exhaust themselves mentally and internally because for most, "self" is their god. Even those who practice religion know that "self" is a constant battle.

There are many parents who don't teach their children about the presence of God. Either they don't know how; or they have an issue with control. Teaching something outside themselves is unfathomable. They decide to supply physical and intellectual needs, but leave out the teaching and example of a life in the Spirit. This is a great disservice to a young mind! Some don't care. If we teach our children to rely on us for everything, what happens when we're no longer around? They'll turn on themselves, thinking they don't have what it takes to make it through life. And they don't! If they did, they wouldn't be born as little babies, needing to be fed and nurtured into adulthood. Our role as parents is to help our children reach the age of accountability with the right provisions for a sound mind - twenty according to the Bible - and turn them over to God for their spiritual growth. We don't kick them out of our lives; but we continue to teach them by example.   Whatever we want them to know, we demonstrate!

If we don't project the joy and peace that comes with sincere belief in a greater good, we set them up for struggle.   Their future may be jeopardized as they struggle to understand their lives in this world.   Granted, there are those who will refuse the idea while fighting for their own individualities.   But once the seeds are sown, God will provide the water and sunshine for their growth.   He takes over eventually, whether we prepare our children or not.   God holds them loosely while they're on a journey toward Him, allowing them the freedom to choose.   Or He holds them tightly while their "ego" is incapacitated by abuse and oppression.   So we hand our children over to God either way.   Parents who raise children with the inconsistencies of their ignorance risk losing their children at the end! All they need to do is to lead them, willingly, through positive, encouraging, and enabling teachings.   Parents are accountable for what they did or didn't do during the formative years of their children.

Obviously many cultures understand the idea of God since there are so many versions of God in the world.   There are twelve major religions: Judaism, Christianity, Islam, Buddhism, Hinduism, Confucianism, Jainism, Shinto, Sikhism, Taoism, and Zoroastrianism. Religion is harmful only if it promotes separation from and judgement of different groups and mentalities.   The common denominator they all possess is the desire to inspire their followers to the enhancement of their souls for salvation and eternal life.   Each set of promises is different.   However, they all present the means for the same purpose: internal peace.

God, through Christ, is my choice.   His promises are as essential to me as food and drink are to my body.   It is through those teachings that I recognize grace and power.   These two form the sustenance of my life.   They heal me and give me the courage to face the unexpected.   I cannot predict the future; nor can I prepare against its variables.   If I don't use God's resources, I'll be shortchanging myself.   And I certainly don't care to overcome everything all by myself.   Though God's focus remains on me a lot more than mine is on Him, my sincere and thankful prayers start a communication of love and unity between the two of us every day. I'm important to Him.

Over the years, I learned that listening to God is difficult because it takes patience.   At the beginning, it was hard for me to sit still, for however long it took, to hear a revelation from Him.   Then there were times I waited on Him for hours, because I believed my need was important.   I was determined not to leave until He gave me something.   Though His message didn't arrive in an audible form; if I listened, I understood the answer.   It surfaced from within.   It blossomed inside of me.   It was an inner voice without the sound. Many successful people have admitted experiences like this, saying, "I don't know why I did that; it was just a hunch."   Each of us who give the worry over to God, have similar moments of awe.   Sometimes, the gift we receive is greater than what we had pictured.

What *is* that inner voice that whispers so gently?   Is it partly "intuition", which is the ability to understand instantly, without conscious reasoning?   If it is, that would make it more powerful than intellect.   It's the knowing without knowing!   But if we take the time to yield to it; instead of ignoring it, the same natural mechanism turns into faint internal whispers; almost as if someone else is breathing words of wisdom into us. The trouble is, those whispers answer our motives. What we do and think and dream regularly proliferates in us. If our focus is "conspiring against others", then the inner voice becomes an encyclopedia of evil plots. The more we practice evil; the more cunning we get. Fortunately, the more we operate with good intentions, those whispers will become the fragrant, cooling breeze of the Holy Spirit, which is the source of all "good." He waits patiently to lead us unto a more dignified path.

God is sovereign over all! And He is holy. When we invite Him, He molds our character to high moral standards. Through a regular life of prayer, He is in constant communion with us. That's what He started in the Garden of Eden. Good personality traits are slow to develop in today's world; but once we learn them, we are able to stand out from all the others. God designed us for important accomplishments. He gave us the "mind" to imagine and to reason with; the "speech" to communicate, and the "intuition" to tap into a hotline of His promptings. He expects the best of us; because He placed that potential in us. He said we are more than conquerors. To paraphrase the Bible, that means "Not only do we achieve victory; but we are overwhelmingly victorious." It's not a one-time thing. It's a lifestyle. If we know God is for us; then who can be against?

What we consider a problem in today's world is an opportunity to see how far we've come. Imagine joining a soccer team; and practicing long gruesome hours to be a part of this great team. But unless we play against the opposing team, we'll never know how good we are. So the match is actually a display of our progress. It's like being graded according to our performance. The sooner we own our capacity to the fullest, the sooner we rise above insecurity, disappointment, or offense.

We must also guard our hearts against negativity. I own a business. At the end of each day I close the register and read the report. I do the same with my soul by listening to its sorrow or its happiness at the epilogue of each day. I make peace with the moments I could've performed better, and I try to learn from my mistakes. I thank God for the ability and the wisdom to recognize joy. This particular time is between Him and me. It's not a "tell all." It's not about reflecting on what others did. I cannot judge someone else's behavior without sounding self-righteous. That's like taking a sledge hammer to the good deeds of my day and smashing them!

God obviously knows everything about me; yet He wants to hear about them from me. He still enjoys my "visit" of reverence and awe just as He did in the Garden of Eden. He wants me to come clean about my wrongs and make amends. My approach for His help, even for the smallest favor, delights Him. He is the Father; and I'm the Child. I can lift my arms and anticipate the palms of His hands holding my body, and engulfing me in His embrace. He hugs me the way I've never been hugged before. He holds me tight, and I feel His love. He doesn't always speak to me in life changing intense sentences. His words can be light and friendly. I hear it all, as long as I'm open to His voice. My tender moments with Him change me more profoundly than the loudest moments of conviction. It is His love that transforms me.

In 1919, the great French impressionist painter, Pierre-August Renoir, died at the age of seventy-four. In the last years of his life, he depended on others to move him around in a wheelchair. He had limited arm movements. Therefore, his assistants scrolled large canvases across a custom made easel so he could paint. The rheumatoid arthritis in his gnarled hands and wasted body gave constant pain. Placing a cloth between his fingers to keep the brush from slipping, Renoir continued to paint until the day he died. When asked why he submitted his body to so much physical pain and suffering, Renoir's response was, "the pain passes, but the beauty remains."

Renoir's life is exactly how God's idea of perfection blossoms. It's formed through suffering. God tells us that He refines us and tests us in the furnace of affliction for His own sake. If we're eager to display a life of our identity rather than God's, we might reject that entire passage from the Bible. Or we'll have a strong reaction saying, "What kind of egotistical and cruel God would test His creation this way?" But refusing to accept something because it goes against our own agenda doesn't take away from its validity. The truth is solid. It stands out no matter what. God doesn't take pleasure in our pain! He allows it because He wants us to be fit for eternal fellowship with Him. God is pure. We cannot remain impure and strive toward our full godly potential at the same time. A surgeon re-breaks a bone in order for it to heal properly. If that makes perfect sense to us, then we should be willing to accept short-term setback for a redemptive purpose.

This world, with all its evil, is God's deliberately chosen

environment for His people to grow in their character. We're not here to stay. We're passing through. We're citizens of Heaven and; while on earth, we are being prepared for our eternal zip code. Therefore, each discomfort, humiliation, and stroke of suffering is God's chisel chipping away everything undesirable. He wants our inner potential to rise and reflect His attributes. Being "born again" means being reconstructed spiritually so we can live a new life of righteousness and obedience. Why should we choose to limp when we can hop, skip, and jump unsurpassably over life's complications?

    God is in complete control of every molecule in the universe at every moment. Everything that happens is either caused or allowed by Him for His perfect plan. His purpose is not to make us feel good; but for us to *be* good. His definition of good and ours are entirely different. Ours would read, "An absence of famine, and drought; poverty, abuse, cancer, and other hurtful afflictions people face all over the world." An entire world free of suffering and challenges would be good; but that's not the case. The more we excel in knowledge and science, the more puzzled we are over new problems we find. Health issues caused by environmental contaminations and emerging infectious diseases are a growing concern worldwide. Our food and water supplies are affected by pesticides and airborne contaminants. We're constantly looking for new solutions for all of that.

    God isn't finding out what's happening as the events unfold. He is in charge of them! Sitting back and watching us struggle doesn't describe Him at all. We don't realize how fascinatingly intricate His plans are for the universe; because our capacity to see and understand is limited next to His.   God is unlimited in power and unrivalled in majesty.   He is the solution for everything.   His storehouse is ready to be unlocked by our heartfelt prayers.   The trouble is, we expect God to give the things we're asking for.   And He does; but not the way we expect.   He assists us as we surge toward the right qualities we need to develop and be fit for an eternal fellowship with Him.

God's gifts are hidden in plain sight, right in the middle of our ups and downs.   If we have the attitude that we are ruined, or broken, or hopeless, then our eyes easily overlook the blessings we've prayed for.   The unseen opportunities will pass us by without notice.   "Manya" was a little Polish girl's nickname.   Manya was stuck under Russian authority, during the 1800's.   She was born to a family of teachers; and she understood the value of learning early on.   Before Manya turned eleven, her eldest sister died of typhus and her mother died of tuberculosis.   As a young teenager, she was hired by the owner of a beet-sugar factory to teach the children of the peasant workers how to read.   On her spare time, a chemist in the beet-sugar factory gave Manya some lessons, because Poles were not allowed in universities then.   Discrimination and poverty couldn't destroy Manya's hidden potential.   They fueled her determination to be the first woman to win a Nobel Prize, not once but twice, in the study of two new chemical elements - radium and polonium.   She carried out the first research into the treatment of tumors with radiation, and she became the founder of the Curie Institutes, the important medical research centers of today.   Madame Marie Curie's contributions in discovering the mysterious presence of "radioactivity" opened a new era for medical knowledge and treatment of diseases.   The pain young Manya suffered as a little girl led her to the determination that helped many to healthier lives.

When she suffered depression after her losses, Manya could've given in to a depressive mentality.   She could've blamed the country, the government, and the system, for all the details missing from her life.   But she didn't.   The year of stagnation as she made peace over the deaths of her family served its purpose.   She marched out of it with fresh determination.   It was time to beat down the odds.   Rising above circumstances gave her a taste of accomplishment and a sense of worth she never had.   Not everyone has the capacity to become a doctor or a scientist.   But I believe a tiny, blessed hand-full fights to find out where they fit in the grand scheme of things.

We have young people today who have all the opportunities for a better education, a more comfortable lifestyle, and the possibility to offer their children far better than the past generations.   Yet they prefer being fed by others.   Some live to qualify for a disability pension so they'll have a guaranteed income.   Others may force the system, bypassing rules and regulations.   Many don't know the definition of "suffering"; yet they suffer from the mentality they've created.   The majority locate a comfort spot and believe they've arrived.   Doing the honorable thing doesn't register.   Yet they are the ones who complain the most about what life owes them!   They've never figured out that "life is what you make."   Admitting fault or responsibility is extinct.   "Self" is god.   Therefore, there's no unity.

Marriages fall apart before the right elements to sustain them are developed.   Businesses dissolve because decision makers can't find a common ground to nurture their investment.   Family dynamics are completely overtaken by greed and resentment.   People are dismissed or disowned for selfish excuses.   And everything is justifiable.   Those who don't want to entertain a relationship with God live in a deranged world of *their* creation.   And I'm not talking about the ritual of going to church every Sunday to warm the pews.   We are carbon copies of past generations.   So what happens when we realize there is more to life?   What if we simply managed to co-exist but never truly lived life?   And the deeper "us" remained dead?   What if we discover too late that there is a spiritual plane we were meant to reach?

    Heaven is cross-cultural.   In Christian and Islamic understanding, heaven is a paradise where the righteous hope to spend eternity.   It is visualized as the Garden of Eden and the World to Come.   According to Confucianism, the Mandate of Heaven bestows authority to a just and virtuous ruler, the Son of Heaven.   In Beijing, the capital of China, Tiananmen is a building that has become a national symbol.   It translates as "The Gate of Heavenly Place".   The Chinese characters used are "heaven", "peace", and "gate".   Jainism describes the Upper World as the World to come where the righteous sit enthroned, with crowns on their heads, rewarded for their deeds.   They enjoy the luster of the Divine Splendor.   Zoroastrianism believes heaven will descend to the moon, and the earth will rise to meet it!   Heavenly forces triumph over evil, rendering it forever impotent!

    We obviously have a huge variety of religious beliefs.   And a great percentage of the world population understands the concept of heaven.   It's a place of timeless harmony where the weary gets to rest.   It's a place of contentment, often described as a "higher place". It's the presence of God; a utopian state.   It's the absence of sorrow, suffering, and sin.   We may not use the same definition, but we all know God is a place of refuge.   And those who need to see to believe ask for evidence.   God is real; and He's waiting to reveal Himself to everyone.   We just need to desire Him over our earthly preferences!

    We don't see the wind, but we know it exists by the rustling of the leaves.   When it is strong, its impact can sway, break, or uproot the tallest tree.   And the trees that survive may have suffered damage in their root-soil contact, causing them long term injury. Since we know the variety of wind, from gentle breeze to destructive cyclone, by their effects we learn to cope with the effects.   The reason our eyes don't see God is not because He makes Himself unavailable or invisible to some.   It's because some people blur their own vision with rubbish.   They believe they know everything, and try to stay blameless at all times.   Or they believe nothing can help them since they're too far gone.   Their unsettling loss of integrity makes those around them gag!   "God must be just as disgusted", they think. These unhappy thoughts are makers of human failure.

    No matter what kind of person we have become, God is always one step away.   All we have to do is turn around and see Him.   The first embarrassing moment in history was when Adam hid behind a fig leaf, thinking God will scold him for his disobedience.   But the Bible says, "God sent him out of the Garden of Eden, lest he reach out his hand and take also of the tree of life and eat, and live forever" (Genesis 3: 22).   Living forever is a gift from God.   But living forever with disobedience was an illness that needed to be cured.   God gave only two instructions.   Adam failed with the first one.   And God stopped Adam before he disobeyed a second time!   He never banished Adam and Eve from His presence.   He only banished them from the perfect garden.   He spared them from their disobedience, the breaking of their promises.   The resolve missing in them needed to evolve under different circumstances.

To this day, God forgives our dysfunctions; but He never abandons us.   Why would He promise us a Savior if He didn't love us?   We are perfect in His sight, if we believe what the Bible says is true; instead of believing what the "world" says is true.   The more we allow God to mold us into His image, the more purpose, meaning, joy, and peace we find.   God erases our afflictions, and we see our true worth!   He designed us for eternal fellowship with Him; and eternal fellowship He will give us!   Our conscience is the mechanism that God created to help us reconnect with our moral sense.   If we choose, it will overthrow our ego; making way for a greater self, which is God.

"You need to have the guidance of someone else.   You cannot train yourself.   I feel the same way about Christianity and about what the Church is: The Church is the gym of the soul", said Sylvester Stallone in an interview.   He told the world that he chooses Jesus as his savior, and Christianity as his faith, with a humble and peaceful expression on his face.   Stallone wrote the script for "Rocky" with the intention of playing the lead role.   He was offered a huge sum for the story, if someone else could have the lead role.   They didn't think Stallone was fit for it.   First, he was a Nobody.   He had a snarl on his face, and slurred speech due to paralysis during birth.

But Stallone refused.   He was sure that this role was about him, and only him.   Nobody could play it better!   It was his life!   The film series grossed more than $1.25 billion at the worldwide box office, making Stallone the celebrity he is today.

Now we know what happens when we don't give up!   Young Stallone was the product of a bad marriage, going from one foster home to another.   His oddly paralyzed face made him an outcast, causing fights, bad grades, and behavior issues at school.   But he never stopped listening to his inner voice that whispered, "Fight!   You deserve better!"   At the end, Stallone looked back and said: "I have great expectations for the future, because the past was highly overrated."   Good for him!

CHAPTER 5.   AMERICA

Philosopher Friedrich Nietzsche said, "What doesn't kill you makes you stronger."   He was right.   My childhood experiences made me more resilient.   I find people who never walked through challenging circumstances are just as stressed; if not more.   Not encountering anything negative throughout life is not only unrealistic; it's not even healthy.   Those dealing with difficult experiences are actually given a chance to develop an ability to cope with future hurdles.   That is the silver lining of a true and realistic life.

I was born in November of 1956.   But, in 1980, I started celebrating a second birthday on April the 10th.   This one is my "re-birthday" when my daughter Iris and I began a new life in America, about six months after her dad had arriver in order to start the immigration process.   This year marks the 36th year in our adopted land where many accomplishments became possible.   The beginning was marred with fears of where we would settle and find food and shelter.   We ended up in a multi-cultural neighborhood, where no one spoke English.   We felt right at home.   Since we survived displacement, every day was another gift.   Being in this marvelous country was already a great privilege.

We were grateful to make it through step one: leaving the homeland behind.   The uneventful and orderly lifestyle of America was appealing.   Chaos wasn't the main theme.   Most people were at ease and very friendly.   They led good, healthy, moral, and ever-improving lives.   They were taught and shown how to live in harmony.   They were multi-cultural and multi-religious; yet they managed to live together without imposing their convictions on one another. They aimed for happiness and a life of dignity without any aggressiveness. Women were free to work and contribute to their household expenses. That gave them a sense of belonging and pride. Men didn't restrict their spouses. They were considered equals. They prospered without the barriers that exist in other civilizations.

The American Dream is about the opportunity to receive a good education, to pursue a career without criticism, and the right to make choices without the restrictions of class, ethnicity, and religion. What impresses me the most is the fact that young people decide for themselves the kind of profession or religion they choose. Unlike other cultures, they are free in their decisions. Their parents or grandparents can't dictate their future, including who and when to marry.

Every evening we would recite the differences of the culture and make mental notes of things we needed to remember. Our one-bedroom apartment wasn't pretty; but that's what we could afford at the time. A few pieces of furniture were donated to us by a nearby Armenian Church. One special piece was a three-legged rectangular table I'll never forget. We propped the side with the missing leg against the wall and it served its purpose. And if we ran into anything at the dumpster that we could use, we weren't too proud to haul. Grocery shopping was the only important task I had during those days. I knew where the cheapest bread, pasta, and hot dogs were. Jello was the choice of dessert. Fresh fruit was too expensive.

The only good thing during that time was that my husband didn't lose his temper as frequently. He was more focused on adapting to this new life where everything was foreign to us both. We were equal to the task.   The unique gift of "unity" descended upon us for the first time; and lasted for about six months, until the novelty wore off.   He was gentle and forgiving during those humbling months.   Then we received our social security cards and all the necessary paperwork saying we could "legally" work and pay taxes. The everyday challenge was different, but we tackled it together. Accomplishments and sorrows were shared.   We laughed together. The ongoing response to personal blunders was, "You're such a refugee!"   I didn't want or anticipate his aggressiveness to return, and I was certainly very thankful for the period of normalcy in our marriage.

    I can't speak for other immigrants but I felt chills of pride each time I heard the Star Spangled Banner.   I was home; and I never longed for the home I left behind.   I escaped all sorts of insanities, and traveled the distance because nothing about my background was more important than what I could offer to my children.   In fact, the only time I spoke up was when my husband mentioned he would consider returning to Istanbul if things didn't work out.   I told him such an option wasn't a possibility for me.   One does not exchange the orphan mentality for a sense of belonging just to see how it might work out.   Nobody goes from a timid newbie to a confident, competent go-getter, without tapping into their inner strength.   The refugee mentality is an extreme level of survival commitment.   It's that "sink or swim" experience.   Learning to be aggressive was an effort for me.   There was no going back!

    I was extremely touched by Anthony Quinn's performance in Nikos Kazantzakis' "Zorba the Greek" as a man with many occupations.

He was a chef, a miner, a storyteller, a musician, and a dancer. He portrayed the lifestyle of the working class whose riches were about appreciating each day and living it fully. He spoke intensely of war, religion, and love. And when the sorrow or the joy became too great to express, he danced, "clapping his hands" as the narrator describes, "pirouetting in the air, falling on to his knees, leaping again with his legs tucked up, as if he was made of rubber." He was a person with multifaceted contradictions. His child-like innocence was anything but naive. His feeble expression showed instant vitality when deep feelings surfaced. Even though he lived in Crete, his native country, he was changed many times due to unexpected circumstances. His approach to life's twists and turns was contagious. His desperate attempt to put the Past to rest rhymed with my life lessons. He inspired me to be a better person.

    Somebody is always watching our steps, evaluating and analyzing us in the great dance of life. If we stop caring about what others think of us, and instead, croon "I did it my way" like Frank Sinatra sang, we too can dance like nobody's watching. We can dance like a child, waving our arms and kicking our legs with abandon, with no fear of judgment. We can twirl weightlessly as if we're orbiting the clouds, with ludicrous expressions of maximum joy. The question is, "Can we hear the music of faith and hope?" We need no instruments for it. We need no facilitators. We need the deepest belief that no opposition can pluck away from its substance.

    Life happens! Looking for meaning can be premature if we are costantly trying to overcome mistakes. And trying to find shortcuts is even a greater nonsense if we haven't learned from those mistakes. The ability to create something from nothing is the great purpose we find when we love and cherish Creation. Our stalwart determination to reach this goal should not arise from a desire to be remembered. It should be about leaving a better DNA for those who look up to us. Though we try to better ourselves, we cannot forget the roots that nurtured us with an urgency to conquer the unpredictable. That's why I admire a refugee mentality. Nothing is handed to you! You *make* it happen; including a sense of belonging. Having one foot in one culture and one in another gives you the wisdom to choose a richer value system. Making it to the United States was a great opportunity for me. And I knew my children would benefit more at the end.

  I love everything about my life here in the United States. I had much to prove, and plenty to mend. I became a naturalized citizen as soon as I qualified. But the distance I put between Armenia and America wasn't far enough to keep me away from oppressive thoughts. I often struggled with darkness and insecurity. Yet they couldn't dilute my determination, because it was no longer about me. My children topped my priority list; and they were my strength at the same time.

  As challenges bounced away and left me on a more dignified path, I found an inner identity that blossomed into the new me. My husband left for unidentified reasons eleven years after we moved to the States. I had waited so long for us to talk about our problems; but I was scared to say anything. I waited silently, until one day, he walked away. I wasn't sad. It was inevitable, because I had changed so much. I no longer crumbled under criticism. Continents away from my mother had given me the freedom to be someone new. The proof of my new self was demonstrated the day my husband slammed the door and walked out. I was calm. In fact, I had never been that calm before. The peace that surrounded me was tangible. I could touch it and I could taste it. It was sweet. The only promise I made to my kids right there and then was the fact that there would no longer be any yelling or screaming in our house. It was time we practiced civilized communication and respected one another's opinions.

There was one problem left to resolve. It was my secret, desperate urge to scream. It wasn't triggered by anger. It had nothing to do with being overwhelmed with certain situations or panicking. It only came to the surface when I was alone and calm. Yet when I opened my mouth, fully prepared to let it all out, nothing happened. I even drove on the highway, all windows rolled down so I could shout. Still nothing! Yet its presence was loud on the inside! It was my internal hell. I didn't know what I was supposed to scream about or who at. Yet I wanted to scream. Either my mind was sending the wrong signal or my voice wasn't responding! Something was out of kilter. I've heard of therapies where people literally scream at the top of their lungs. It can go on for minutes or hours, depending on the person or the need. I never went to one of those; but I wondered.

I thought of hiking to the top of a mountain and letting my screams challenge the wind! Their echoes could have tricked my mind and helped me release every bit of them. I wished there was a safe place for broken people to go when it's too much. Where we can burst at the seams and fall apart for a while. Everyone would be equal regardless of his reality; the only common denominator being their occasional silent meltdown. We may appear fine due to the illusion of control; but deep inside, things are raging at times. We choose repression over depression because it's our only hope to keep life presentable.

My beliefs and behaviors from the past changed tremendously; but burying the memories involves a part of the brain I don't know how to access. They don't impair me on a regular basis; but I'm reminded of them now and then, when something unpleasant dispirits me. The effort to drown the unpleasant in happier thoughts is no longer huge task. Not to mention the fact that they visit me less and less. My optimism whacks them when necessary. I constantly leave the past behind for a better future.

I don't know how long it was before my divorce was final. I forgave him for everything; but I never wanted to see him again. He was my first love. And he broke my heart. But I knew divorce isn't a license to hate; especially when I have two beautiful kids from that marriage. They too needed help processing their sadness. I feel for parents who are steeped in anger and won't let it go. They use their children to hurt the other parent. Buddha said, "Holding on to anger is like grasping a hot coal with the intent of throwing it at someone else. You are the one who gets burned." The longer we hold on to unpleasant memories of the past, the longer it will take to create a victorious future.   The optimum result comes when we stop blaming the other person, and identify *our* responsibility for the failed relationship.   This approach is not to point the finger at someone; it's to learn from previous choices, and make better choices so we won't repeat the past.

Recognizing *why* a marriage should end is more important than *how* it should end.   We must take the time to think what kind of harm our children have to endure.   My mother told me the reason she never divorced my father was because of us kids.   I guess she was trying to compare me to herself, and explain why she was a better mother.   I looked straight into her eyes and said, without flinching, "I divorced because of my kids.   They deserve a better home."   Her digs didn't stop there.   "We'll never be complete until you have a man sitting next to you at the table", she would say.   She found a new scab to pick.   She never thought before she spoke.   But I wondered about all the times when she walked to the altar for communion, she wore a head cover made of lace.   That's a symbol of ascending the ladder of sanctity.   Of course, she's not the only hypocrite in the body of organized religions.   But we must understand that hypocrites are never a part of the body of Christ!   God is the Gardener who weeds us and feeds us so He can bring us to our best bloom.   The weeds are plucked and burned!

My life as a single parent started with a healthy relationship with God.   He was the head of my household.   Even though I knew I was the breadwinner, He was in charge of my life.   I prayed He would multiply my income and enlarge my territory. I prayed He would look after my kids while I was providing for them. According to statistics, children who grow up with one of their parents are twice as likely to drop out of high school, or two-and-a-half times as likely to become teen parents versus children who grow up with both parents. I knew trying to be everything for them was impossible. I couldn't be at home for them and at work at the same time. I couldn't be everything. I had to stop worrying about their wellbeing. If I wasn't at peace with a circumstance, I knew I hadn't prayed enough about it. So I prayed until my concerns died down. I got rid of my sleep disorder that way! One prayer took care of that problem when three different prescription sleep aids had failed! I stopped waking up every couple of hours, thinking it was time to go to work. I slept like a baby throughout the night, and every night thereafter, after "one" heartfelt prayer.

My business was very important. It provided for my family as well as my parents for whom I had filed petition to become a part of this great country. I make it a priority and asked my kids not to call unless it was an emergency. My daughter was very respectful of my request. My son was too young to think of anyone else at the time. He would start leaving a message on the answering machine with, "Mom! This is an emergency...". He did have a problem with patience; that's all. Both kids were my strength; my reason to be. They still are.

There was no time to waste. Years went by quickly. I promised never to complain, and God continued to provide for my business. I've known many hard working individuals. Working hard wasn't enough.   There had to be divine help sending opportunities to be used, and the right people to lead the way.   Help comes when needed.   The more I learned to depend on God, the more He surprised me.   There is a tremendous difference between "knowing about God" and actually "knowing God."   Many people are turned away by the idea of Him, because they've never trusted what He can do.   They're either self-sufficient or impatient.

    I am not exceptional.   I was humble because of my upbringing.   I lacked self-confidence and self-respect.   I had not tasted the generosity of God.   In fact, "self" was mutilated at a young age.   So there was plenty of space in my heart for God to fill. I never knew "desperate" would bring me to my knees.   And on my two knees, I opened the door to my heart for my God.   I was patient, because I only knew how to be the last and the least.   By the time I mixed those two ingredients, there was that sweet perfume that rose heavenward to get God's attention.   Our humility is always a sweet fragrance to Him.   He takes delight in it.   Now that I'm seeing results, I'd like to thank Mom for introducing me to the Parent she never knew.

    Khalil Gibran said, "Wisdom ceases to be wisdom when it becomes too proud to weep, too grave to laugh, and too selfish to seek other than itself."   Losing self means to let go of worry about the future or disappointment about the present.   It allows us to identify with others.   As we feel one with those who need our care, we find that we can make a difference by doing God's work!   Expecting to be recognized or the favor to be returned is selfish.   In fact, if we calculate how we might benefit, our focus hinders the spontaneous intuition of our heart.   We must "pay-it-forward!"   That's the gift that keeps giving.   Helping others with the right intention expands our identity.   Only then is it released from its confinement, and overflows with volume and capacity.

The art of giving is not bound in nature.   It's a process.   A baby who is looked after and taught the necessities early on should return the grace by contributing during his full potential as an adult. According to the Bible, the age of accountability is twenty.   That's when we're no longer considered a dependent.   That's when we are to become benefactors to our surroundings.   The more selfless we try to become the more unhindered we are by the results.   That is ultimate freedom!   Thoughts like "What if they don't appreciate my efforts?"   "I can't believe they didn't even notice!" or "I'll never do that again!" will be banished from our path.   We will be disengaged from disappointments, yet still be connected to the world where we find many fulfillments for our hearts.

We weren't designed to be alone.   We were meant to interact.   And the greater the harmony emanating from us, the greater harmony we find within.   Many cultures explain this differently; but it's all the same meaning.   Turks say, "etme bulma dunyasi"; meaning you reap what you sow in this world.   According to Jainism, people are born and born again until they rid themselves of negative karmic substance.   The Buddhism teaches people to minimize karma's negative impact by leading a righteous life.   Hindus promote "what goes around comes around."   And the Bible says on the subject, "Do not be deceived: God cannot be mocked.   A man reaps what he sows.   Whoever sows to please their flesh, from the flesh will reap destruction; whoever sows to please the Spirit, from the Spirit will reap eternal life" (Galatians 6: 7- 8).   But I like this one best, "They sow the wind and reap the whirlwind." (Hosea 8: 7) Right to the point!

I'm not into futurism.   I barely grasp today's facts.   I watch most of the Sci-Fi features with my kids because they enjoy them.   I remember getting into this one movie called "The Matrix."   And this is what I got from it: at some point humans lose a war to machines, and they take over our lives.   But they need power to stay alive; so they use us as batteries.   Thinking they need to keep us docile, they leave us to dream in a world they created called The Matrix. However, some of us see past the dream and understand the truth. We may escape and live in the dystopian future, but we will be hunted by machines.   Morpheus, one of those fugitives, asks Neo, also known as The One, "What is real?   Only that which you can smell, touch, or taste? Then 'real ' is electrical signals interpreted by your brain!"   He also says, "Neo, sooner or later you're going to realize that there's a difference between knowing the path and walking the path".   I never imagined I could relate to a futuristic movie until this one.   It told its audience there's more to life, and unless we participate in the journey, we miss out on the potential.

During the first half of life, our choices are influenced by genetics and culture.   They're set by parents, teachers, or love interests.   And one day, we're awakened to the truths by which we've lived, and realize that their opposites also contain truth.   We stay busy in an effort to avoid questions for which we fear there may be no answers.   So, we feed our insatiable appetite with amusement and addiction: our profession, social events, computers and cell phones. All the psychological needs remain undeveloped because of all the distractions. Think about it. We have access to the ultimate high; yet we exchange it for a shadow. What we need to do is pray and meditate. Procrastinating and avoiding the subject is not going to get rid of it. It's going to delay our potential.

An unlived life will go unidentified and unrecognized. Whatever we dislike about ourselves, we will criticise and chastise in others. What we lack in ourselves, we'll depend on others to provide. We might infest others with our fears and insecurities. Though they cannot be removed completely, those lessons will be tempered, allowing our unlived potential to emerge fully and constructively. Why let others control our destiny when we can be in charge? How often do we pretend, and then pretend we're not pretending? Those are mind games we play to camouflage the *real* sensitive subjects inside.

Everything I went through happened so I could become a better me. Life wasn't against me. If I had lost control of my life, it could have consumed me. Yet it had no control over my thoughts and how I processed things. I deeply believe that my basic fundamentals were the right ones. And holding on to them was the right thing to do. That's what determined how tall I walked. And I was pretty stubborn about it. As I wrote earlier, there comes a time we start giving back. My attitude was not determined by what life offered. If so, I would definitely be a passive aggressive individual. "What attitude do I bring to life?" is the real question.

My future is what I think it will be. If I speak positively and credulously, I will continue to plant the right seeds into my life. And the more control I exercise over my feelings, the more speed I'll have in the progress of my life. The mind is the most powerful force in existence. It can eject the unthinkable as long as I don't limit myself. Someone's IQ is a flimsy measure of intelligence to teach us about our potential future. Yet our potential won't detonate unless it's exposed to internal pressure. Such pressure forces a glitch in the brain that empowers a part of it to soar above the human normal. Most geniuses were told, as children, they would never amount to anything.

I may be considered an over-thinker; but I know I'm not a genius. I simply have good reason to believe that life couldn't swallow me, because it was preparing me for higher purposes. If I believe that, then no matter how small my progress, I will plan my next venture so I can create a chain reaction of wonderful! With practice and discipline, I will direct my thoughts towards my goals and dreams. I've been in America for over three decades. And I've been given opportunities that were impossible in my previous life. Today, I know not to waste a moment of this miracle called "life" and, to make every moment count. We're not here to compare apples and oranges as a way to scornfully review the work of others. But we are here to present our best work, so others will be inspired.

CHAPTER 6.   BLESSINGS

Single parenthood was scary at the beginning.   Nobody prepared me for it.   It's not that my kids were difficult.   I just didn't trust myself.   Until my divorce I was confused, submissive, and withdrawn.   I was passive all my life.   How could I act for my children when I had never acted for myself?   I only knew to accept and follow others' decisions.   Now I had to make sound decisions.   I had to defend my family.   Fighting on the front line was not my thing.   I hadn't trained for the part.   I was afraid I would shame my children and let them down.

Passivity births a sense of helplessness; which in turn feeds depression and anxieties.   I knew I was overly cautious.   But I couldn't help it.   I was afraid to take action.   If and when the kids made any suggestion, I always said, "Aw, that sounds great... but let's just wait and see."   One day my daughter Iris, thirteen at the time, asked, "What are we waiting for, and what will we see?"   I got quiet. I didn't have an answer.   But I knew I couldn't stall my responsibilities any longer.   I must live up to my children's expectations.   I was comfortable in my rut so far.   But things needed to change.   My kids deserved a parent they could look up to.   I was angry at myself for not figuring this any sooner.   It seems that Iris understood it better than I did.

All children are intuitive; but Iris was highly so.   She was aware of my confusion.   Though I knew she suppressed many of her comments during those days; she never stopped respecting me.   My interpersonal limitations were obvious to her.   She knew my marriage was oppressive. She chose to help me so we wouldn't go back to that awful chapter. She was mindful of my needs and instructions. She watched after her nine-year-old brother, Osheen, until I came home. I had asked them to give me thirty minutes to change into something comfortable and to unwind. Osheen, as usual, had no patience. Iris would be yelling at him, "It hasn't been thirty minutes yet!" She was my greatest supporter, after Dad.

My brain was in "fight or flight" mode all the time. I developed a sleep problem. Falling asleep was easier than staying asleep. I floundered in bed for what seemed like eternity during those nights. If I was lucky enough to fall asleep in the wee hours of the morning, I woke up two hours later, feeling as if I had slept for days. Going back to sleep was out of the question. That little patch of sleep wasn't restful at all. I needed help. I turned to doctors and medications. That didn't help. Then I listened to a self-hypnosis tape I found in a health food store. It gave me the worst nightmare of my life. I dreamed of my kids being tortured by total strangers while I was tied to a post. Their bone-chilling sounds of anguish tormented me for days after that. It was terrifying. I tried the tape a week later. The same effect! This time they were being stabbed in my kitchen as I was immobilized by the intruders. It was so vivid that I ran down the stairs, with a baseball bat in one hand, and went through the whole house to make sure we were safe.

As I walked back into my bedroom that night, something happened. Something that I had never encountered before! First I looked around to see what it was. The room looked the same. My sheets were strewn across the mattress just as I had left them. My un-fluffed pillows were topsy-turvy, displaying my nightmare struggle. But the peace that filled the room was surreal. It didn't rhyme with my experience at all. I never felt this calm before. Never! And I wasn't going to let it go. Either there was a holy presence in my room; or I was being sanctified and reprogrammed. I felt as though my incubus of a life was about to have the "closed" sign up on its door.

 I knelt by the bed. I remained in silence for a time. Didn't utter a word! The deafening silence had its own sound. My mind needed to adjust to its harmony. A captivating scent aroused my attention. It wasn't a perfume I recognized. This one appealed to my inner senses. It calmed me. It birthed the virtue of tranquility. Even my breathing changed. Air wasn't just rushing in and out as a physical necessity. It was slow and lingering; it refreshed my inner chambers like a glass of cool lemonade in the heat of summer. It had a sweet taste. I shut my eyes. The effects were intensified. A mysterious chanting emerged, ever so gently, from the inner cells of my body. I was still being obedient. I knew nothing like this experience before. But I knew it was "good."

 I made a pact that night. Obedience was a specialty of mine. I would learn obedience to the right source. God was to be the head of my household. And I would follow Him without a question. All three of us deserved a better leader. And I already knew I wasn't the one. The only thing I did well was to earn money. So I worked! I became a good provider. My pain and disappointment took a nosedive; and joined my nonexistent ego. My heart grieved in secret. I had to be solid for my kids. What strength I had to work with didn't leave room for resentment, impatience, or eagerness. Trivial issues and vanity had to go. Rock bottom was not an option. This old critter had lived there for a good portion of her life already. She knew all too well about that swampy place!

When you tell God you will follow Him; you may want to snap on the seat belt. From that moment on, my new life was arduous. There were no shortcuts. Each step was vital; and I tried to keep up with His pace. I was like a toddler learning to walk. Dad supported me through the entire process, as usual. Mom's disappointment was obvious. She didn't approve of separation or divorce; but she wasn't the one who suffered for so many years either. Jirayr's admiration continued. He was proud of me one way or the other. This was new for everyone; so we didn't talk about it. It was just another important issue that got swept under the rug. We avoided the subject. Were we expecting the estranged husband to return? Or would the traumatized wife possibly reconcile? None of that happened. I hiked up my own path. I did my best.

A divided family wasn't my goal; but making it healthy again sure was. Kids don't thrive in a troubled family. I wanted to see mine grow up in a happy and stable environment. They were to come home from school and *feel* at home. They could choose their own activities instead of being micromanaged. I encouraged them to use the entire house instead of withdrawing to their rooms all the time. If they ate a snack right before dinner, that was okay too. It took a while. We adapted. And as parents going their separate ways, we didn't wish each other ill. At least I know I didn't. My focus was on the children. The other pieces of the puzzle would come later. There was no hurry.

My kids were the main theme. They still are! Each time I felt overwhelmed with my new assignment as a "single mom", I plunged into the memories of their birth. I still treasure the moments I saw those two precious faces for the first time. That evoked pleasant impressions of "who" I was first and foremost. I was twenty-two years old when I gave birth to my daughter, Iris. She was three weeks early. I thank God for her timing. Patience wasn't easy at that point. I needed her like I needed water to survive the desert. I was parched internally. A new life meant a new beginning. She couldn't change my circumstances. But she would give me a reason to outlive wickedness and depravity.

For months, I had wondered what she would look like or how she would sound. Would she know me right away? Would she recognize my voice? The anticipation was priceless. Touching my belly gave me a connectedness unlike any other. This was a unity I would design and lead. I will teach the simplest, yet most powerful concepts like "love," "kindness," and "generosity." If I didn't have the courage to express what I was made of before, it was time to muster it now. I had to bring forth an attitude of trust and acceptance for this little baby to feel right at home.

The day Iris was born didn't go as expected. It never does. But things rolled quickly once we made it to the hospital. Shortly after we were assigned to a private quarter, her screams filled the room. There she was at last! Her cone-shaped head, baby acne, and puffy eyelids were the first things I noticed. Either disappointed or angry, she was red in the face. Even her disheveled dark hair was in an uproar. I couldn't believe she was inside of me all that time. I counted the toes and the fingers. She was wailing. Naturally and undoubtedly of course, she was the most beautiful baby I'd ever seen. In fact, until they placed her against my chest, all swaddled and calm, I believed all babies were cute. But no longer! From that day forward, they all looked like they weren't quite ready!

When Iris came home from the hospital, I embarked on a new journey. She became my greatest love; a love I never experienced before. And I didn't mind paying the price for this one. She could dictate to me all she wanted! In fact, she fussed often from hunger or if her diaper needed a change. She tormented me night after night with sleep deprivation. She demanded attention twenty-four-seven. There were no limits to my devotion. Affection overflowed from every cell and every fiber. All she had to do was look my way with those innocent eyes. I vouched to provide all of her needs, preserve her purity, and protect her from harm. She was never to experience confusion or anguish under my care. Her tiny presence became my strength and a fresh purpose in life.

Her skin felt like silk. Though small in size, she was a giant in her demands! Since I knew nothing about parenting, I studied her every move. I kept a close watch on the creases of her pout. The quivering of her perfectly shaped lips reached an aria of screams quickly; especially when she was fed up with my ignorance. Either I wasn't fast enough or I hadn't fed her enough. She was an outstanding opera singer though. The music of renowned composers such as Bach, Beethoven, or Zimmer wasn't as thrilling. We had more musical movements at home. Iris' arms and legs acted as the maestro to the symphony she conducted. Her slower movements delivered a smooth sonata.   Those allowed me enough time to figure out what was about to happen.   I feared the ones that made her look as if she was drowning; as if her entire body was fighting to stay afloat. They were accompanied with sharp piercing cries.   They threw me into a state of chaos.   The minute I held her in my arms, she stopped!

I was her only audience, swayed by her performance.   She was the image of perfection to me.   I even loved the "Watch me scream at the top of my lungs" voice.   In time, I found no difference between her toothless little smile, and her wide open screaming mouth!   My initial intimidation was replaced by harmonious habits. I learned to enjoy our boisterous exchanges as a personal concerto. She was the conductor, the orchestra, and the symphony in which I submerged myself, and reached for the heights of unknown measures. She fulfilled me.   I was in awe of her.

Often I went without food or water, because she was all I wanted to eat and drink.   I served all of her needs.   I had none.   I adopted her habits.   I looked for patterns.   I listened to her sounds, especially while breastfeeding.   She went at it with an eagerness you could hear from across the room.   Her eyes and hands would be fixed on my breast as if she was blowing a ginormous balloon.   Her "kha...kha...kha..." sounds were delightful.   I knew she enjoyed her banquet.   Then I held her against my shoulder and burped her.   She rarely had a problem with indigestion.   She had good appetite.   I prayed for enough milk to keep up with her.

Our best time together was when I exercised her.   I laid her on her back and bicycled her legs.   She was a cooing and gurgling machine then. She mimicked my facial expressions. She responded enthusiastically to my "woos" and giggles. I seized the moment every time. She was the most precious gem in the world to me. She made me want to be a better person. I knew I wasn't experienced. But I loved her more than myself. She was the meaning I'd been waiting for.

I was curious about one thing. What would her first word be? Would she say "mama" and make me the happiest? I wanted her to call me by that title so much that I helped her memorize it. I would slowly bring my face close to hers and whisper, "Ma...Ma..." I practiced it while I was spoon feeding her, hoping that she would repeat it before her next spoon-full. She wasn't interested. She had a mind of her own. One day, she started saying a word that baffled everyone: "goat, goat, goat!" This was her first word! It had no meaning in Turkish, nor in Armenian. Iris was being politically correct. She didn't want to hurt anybody's feeling. She came up with a neutral word; a word that meant something only to her little self. I was wild about hearing an entire sentence out of her mouth, filled with countless versions of the same word.

As a toddler, her greatest possessions were her many stuffed animals. She carried them everywhere. She transported them in the proper order, one by one, before nestling herself at the foot of our bed every night. She would not grace her pillow until her entourage was situated just right. You could already tell she was a caregiver from the way she carried her precious possessions with love and tenderness. She was a planner and an organizer. Her little system never changed. The same predictions remain true today. Her disposition is just as unique.   She has her own way of handling issues.   And that's *so* her.   She doesn't bother about doing or saying what is expected of her.   Her right and wrong have a good balance.   I wouldn't change a thing.   I love the way she turned out.   She is everything I wasn't.   She has exceeded all my limitations; whether it be the narrow opinions of my formative years, or the fact that I didn't know how to fight back.   There are countless victories I get to live through her everyday life now these days.

      She called me one day to let me know that she had quit her job.   I was baffled.   I didn't see it coming.   Her explanation was simple.   "You taught me once", she said, "that if I didn't walk away from something I already knew wasn't good enough for me, I wasn't really stepping out in faith".   I didn't know what to say.   I was trying to remember how and when I conveyed that message.   I was silent for a few seconds, trying to process what I had just heard.   Seeing that I needed more explanation, she announced that she was planning to visit me for a week.   "This is the most perfect time to get away before I start my new job", she said.   She was referring to the job she didn't even have yet.   Again, I was speechless.   She truly believed every note of her new sonata.   I needed to journey with her on her walk of faith.   As I collected my thoughts, I praised her wisdom.   I didn't remember giving her that advice; but there were many things I didn't remember due to stress during those days.   Plus, there was nothing to argue.   She was coming home for a week!   I was delighted.

      The few days that she had set aside to visit me brought several opportunities to question her plans for another job.   But I didn't want to interfere with her unique "faith journey". So I chose not to be invasive. Each person's inner enlightenment is bright and designed to feed *that* individual. Even though Iris acquired that advice from me, it didn't come back to me the same way! In fact, I would've never quit a job unless I had a guaranteed replacement! I could kick myself in the rear end for blabbing such nonsense!

On her second day in town, Iris received a phone call from a well-known establishment, inviting her for an interview. She arranged to meet with them after her stay with me. I couldn't believe my eyes, nor my ears. She was cool as a cucumber. Her dignified manner and effortlessness could teach me a thing or two. Then I realized I could start looking up to her just as she had looked up to me all those years. Who knows, I may even learn a thing or two watching her life unfold, as she prepares to play one more movement of her new symphony. She did get the job! And yes, it offered her more money, better conditions, and opportunities than the previous one. She had done the right thing after all!

As I relived this incident during the following weeks, a deeper lesson graced me. I once believed life had been unfair to me, and had cheated me out of many favorable circumstances. I had built a fortress of self-absorption, making sure that the walls were high enough so no one could come in, or out! And, if that wasn't silly enough, I sulked over the fact that no one made the preposterous effort to climb over, demolish it, and free me. As I started forgiving life for all of the miseries it tried to handicap me with, not only was I giving myself a chance to heal; but I was also watching life make it up to me through my own child.

The walk down Memory Lane couldn't possibly be complete without mentioning my second love, my son. When I got pregnant with Osheen, my marriage was already a disappointment. As I was undergoing treatment for a female health issue, I discovered I was with child. I couldn't grasp it! I had been praying to get better without a surgery. I was so happy that my problem was gone. And now I was coming home with a bonus from the doctor's office. I loved him from the moment I knew he was within my body. Now I had two reasons to become a better person!

Such unconditional love transforms one's life. That's what happened for me! So I made it a priority over my ongoing marital issues. My husband had an anger problem due to his insecurity, jealousy, and greed; none of which I could fix. He was a display of different sets of dysfunction. I was barely able to sort through my own. My positive approach irritated him even more. It folded the yeast of hatred into his speech. His ego needed constant flattery; while I was barely coping with the demands of my pregnancy. I didn't know what pained him more. Was it the past? Was it his marriage to me? I had to tune it all out! I could see there were no exit signs on the road ahead.

The growing unrest of my marriage increased food cravings! As the birth approached, I looked and felt fat. And stressed! I was trapped behind an enormous human blanket. I could see others; but could they really see me? At that point, I pledged to give my newborn my best, and I prayed that my daughter Iris, this new baby and I would somehow make it to the shore as a family. I also hoped to give birth to a giant baby, so I wouldn't have to diet for long. Of course that didn't happen. Osheen was premature by two months and extremely tiny. He weighed three pounds and fourteen ounces. I was struck with blame! But as soon as I held him in my arms, I placed all three of us in God's hands, and the cool rain of His grace took all of my concerns away. He was beautiful, and he was mine.

Osheen looked like a baby porcupine. A very cute one! I had to knit a few outfits for him during his stay of twenty-four days at the hospital. Everything was too big for him. I visited every day to breastfeed him. Thank God, he didn't have any health issues. He was small, but he would catch up. He needed to put on weight so we could bring him home. He was quieter than Iris. In fact, he didn't fuss over anything except food! He was a picky eater. I often sang and danced to distract him. He reached the ideal weight within eight months. So by the time he was a year-old baby, no one could tell he was a preemie.

Feeding Osheen was like pulling teeth. His mind was elsewhere. Each time I approached him with food, he wanted to play. He didn't like being interrupted. He had a vivid imagination. His playing was like mine: quiet and undisturbed. Only then did I realize why my little feet had been tied to a table when I was a little girl. I must not have had much of an appetite. I probably would have played my imaginary games without interruption as well. And Mom's idea of a healthy baby was a fat one. She had wanted to fatten me up so I looked the part. Yet I used gentler ways to interest Osheen. I entertained him with gestures and happy stories. Since he had a great imagination, the best thing to do was to feed his imagination as well as his baby tummy. One moment, we prepared for battle, and planned to incapacitate the enemy with a plan of action; or we bulldozed an entire neighborhood and erected massive skyscrapers with our construction crew. I was the screenwriter, just as I had been with my brother Jirayr. That's how I fed Osheen. Often I would say, "one more...and no more!" Ten to fifteen repetitions later, he would finally catch on saying, "You said that already!" Our mealtimes were loving and gentle. This was the right way! My children were never forced to eat anything they didn't like. I encouraged them to smell and taste new foods, and what worked, worked!

Osheen's obsession was his pillow. He wouldn't part from it. I had to wait for him to fall asleep so I could wash the pillowcase. Otherwise he threw temper tantrums and couldn't sleep. His screams seemed infinite, and I hoped our neighbors weren't thinking child abuse was taking place. Visitors annoyed Osheen too. He didn't like strangers in the house. He hid behind a large plant and cried his eyes out until our guests felt bad and left. He wasn't like that with other kids. He just didn't want grown-ups to come over. I wished I could understand what frightened him so much. Did he have secrets I didn't know? Years later, he remembered an awful event that had scarred him for life. His father had cornered him while I was at work one day and he was hitting Osheen on the face, saying, "You're not going to cry! If you do, I will hit you harder!" I found out about this event not too long ago. I guess that was his father's way of making a man out of Osheen. Parenthood is a noble privilege some people don't know to appreciate. Their hunger for power overrides the most intimate relationship they could ever experience. Osheen became a bodybuilder in his adult life. His muscular body intimidates many; but he's made sure he'll never be intimidated.

He tells me I'm his role model, since his father left the marriage when both kids were very young.   Through his eyes, I am the one who taught him how to be a gentleman.   And he wonders how this was possible.   My answer was simple.   "If grandpa could teach me how to be a lady; I can teach you how to be a gentleman." After all, Dad would be happy to know his qualities were passed down regardless of all the surrounding negativities.

Laughter and smiles are the greatest legacy one can leave. They uplift us!   They keep our attitude positive and inviting; which tells the world we're not crumbling any time soon.   I somehow had this inscribed into me long time ago.   Eleanor H. Porter's fictional character "Pollyanna" and I were best buds.   After both her parents died, Pollyanna was sent to live with her only relative, a reclusive and stern aunt.   To everyone she met, Pollyanna explained "the glad game" that her father taught her before he died.   He taught that no matter what happens, there's always something to be glad about. And when she received a pair of crutches as a gift one Christmas morning, her father told her, "be glad about the crutches, because you don't need to use them."   Pollyanna brought so much gladness to her aunt's dispirited town that she ended up transforming it into a pleasant place to live.   I also became numb to life's countless disappointments because of Dad's teachings.   I drew strength from them, as if each one was a higher rank or a bigger medal to earn.

A positive perspective accompanied with humility and

gratitude is a direct path to inner peace.   We can certainly remedy life's unpleasant details with it.   Focusing on what's right instead of what's wrong keeps our thoughts light.   We cannot always act and sound optimistic; especially when we experience pain and discomfort. We have to be honest with ourselves.   And we have to be honest with those who care about us.   We must give them the opportunity to minister to us.   A simple heart-to-heart can be very uplifting. There is room for sadness now and then.   And occasional tears serve a purpose too; as long as we diffuse the pity-party at some point with something that we appreciate regardless about our situation.

Everybody searches for happiness these days.   There is an intense pursuit for it.   If we can't reach it one way, we'll try something else.   What people don't seem to know is that finding happiness is a skill.   We acquire that skill by using the ability to see something good in everything.   Something to be thankful for. Something that will minimize unpleasantness without ignoring it. This is not natural for mankind.   Yet with practice, it can become second nature.   Hardships and tough seasons of life are guaranteed. Even hardship can be managed through a good perspective.   We either give in to worry and complain our lives away; or we move forward thinking, "This too shall pass.   It's only temporary."   When things are going our way, we must enjoy them, because there will come a day when they won't be going our way.   And when we're going through tough times, we must remember that it won't last forever; and that we'll eventually get through it.

Joslin was one of five children born in 1939 to an alcoholic father.   He suffered from low self-esteem due to sexual abuse from the age of six to thirteen. He escaped by enlisting in the Air National Guard, but was discharged due to a head injury. He decided to prepare a paper while in college that would examine the historical evidence of the Christian faith, so he could disprove it. He was an agnostic and couldn't fathom the presence of a God who approved the suffering of innocent children. Instead, he found evidence *for* Christianity, not against it. So Josh McDowell, the real name of the voiceless victim he once was, began his speaking and writing ministry to inspire and teach youth. His struggles helped place proper focus relationships and sexual mores. Today, he is known for his seminars, debates, and books in Christian apologetics. He has spoken across the United States, and in other nations including the Republic of South Africa and Australia. Josh McDowell is also the founder of Josh.com and Operation CareLift, both designed to meet physical and spiritual needs in orphanages, hospitals, schools, and prisons in the countries of the former Soviet Union. He has received two significant honors from the Russian people because of those efforts. Josh Mc Dowell was nominated 36 times for the Gold Medallion Award and received that award on four occasions.

    Evil doesn't stand a chance in the presence of Good. I know it took a long time and a lot of effort to heal his horrific childhood, but Josh McDowell proved to the world that it can be done. I wish the world could become what we see through rose-colored glasses. We all want to look through them! They enhance our reality as well as our imagination. They could make the world a place where people would love and uplift one another. Unity and commitment would be lasting. Individuals working together could easily make a flawless future. They would step on grace and walk in integrity. They could speak what they mean; and mean what they say!   A handshake and a promise would be enough to bind a relationship.   We could all outdo each other with our good deeds and prefer giving over receiving; in lieu of trying to take advantage of every person and every situation.

That is the world many of us would love to see!   Yet it's only a dream today.   We're still struggling with greed and selfishness.   We failed God's standards at the Garden of Eden; and now we're failing ours.   Just when we think we can't get any worse, we stoop even lower.   The forbidden fruit wasn't the problem.   It was made by perfection Himself.   Yet some commentators and evangelists have focused on "why" the tree was there in the first place.   Like God should've polled our opinions before He planted it!   Didn't He already know we would fail?   Was it a set up?   Why didn't God direct His anger toward Eve?   She was the one who failed the command!   Would it have easier for the world to understand what really happened if God had asked Adam and Eve not to touch a certain old spare tire instead of the fruit from that particular tree?   The problem was the disobedience; and it came from us.   God never failed us.   We failed Him!   And God, in His infinite wisdom and mercy, took us out of His perfect presence until we desired to be more like Him; and chose His ways over our temptations.   Those earliest biblical stories set the stage for The Great Flood, the destruction of a flawed world, and the cleansing for the next phase of God's Creation.   The Book of Genesis is a powerful first chapter in God's Book!   In it, there is nothing that we couldn't possibly understand; unless we're dead set against understanding it.

God's love for us is so unconditional that His forgiveness is always greater than our flaws.   Like sound-minded parents would want to teach their children good character traits; God too nurtures men and women to grow in holiness.   We were once given a chance by the Master, and we blew it!   Adam was the most perfect example of today's mentality when he started saying, "The woman you gave me..."   He was actually dumb enough to hold God responsible for what took place in the Garden.   And not much has changed since then.   We still take full credit for our accomplishments.   And we blame God for the lack of them.   That is of course, if we're smart enough to understand the universe didn't birth itself into existence; but God, in His infinite wisdom, created all things to function in harmony and perfection.

    We still reject God's teachings.   The Bible is available to everyone.   Those who own a copy hardly make the time to read it.   They make up excuses or won't even bother with any.   And we complain about the dysfunctions of humanity, our homes, our government, our world, etc.   Pointing a finger at something or someone else doesn't lessen our shame.   If we're older than twenty, we have already reached the age of accountability.   That means God has given us new things to focus on; whether it be a family, a profession, or a special purpose.   The nasty memories of our past cannot be buried overnight; but we must not use them as an excuse, or dwell on them for attention.   I feel sad for those who hold on to their memories like a trophy they've won.   They show them off every chance they get.   What they're really doing is holding on to them; because it's the only reality they know.   And since the unknown frightens them more, moving forward is out of the question.

Everyone has heard and read about Sodom and Gomorrah, the two cities mentioned in the Bible, the Torah, and the Quran, where the divine judgment of God came down as fire and brimstone, and consumed everyone.   They're still used as metaphors for wickedness and sexual immorality.   Abraham's nephew, Lot and his wife and two daughters were allowed to escape God's wrath because of Abraham's supplications.   Angels took hold of Lot's hand, his wife's hand and his daughters', and brought them out of the city.   They told them to move forward and never look back.   And Lot's wife, Ado or Edith in some translations, a native of Sodom, looked back and became a pillar of salt.   We'll never know why she looked back.   It could've been empathy.   Knowing she was leaving two of her daughters behind, it was more like "one last look" before she left. The night before, when the angels graced Lot's house, she didn't show them hospitality.   She was annoyed with her husband for asking her to bring "salt" to the table.   So she went door to door telling the neighbors that her husband was ignoring the laws of the city by inviting strangers.   She had an opportunity to entertain angels in her home; but she turned the entire evening into a disaster over salt!

One of the angels held her hand the next morning and helped her escape with the family.   Her defiance against her husband was forgiven, because of God's promise to Abraham.   But her fate was sealed when she disobeyed God.   There is so much we need to learn about this subject.   I wish there was an "undo" button in life. Wouldn't it be great if we could erase our past embarrassments?   Or retract hurtful words?   Or mend broken hearts?   Mistakes are accompanied by consequences.   And tomorrow doesn't always come. All we have is this moment in time to do the right thing, to act the right way, and to leave the right legacy. We weren't given a handbook to parent our children. But God's parenting came with one: The Bible.

    I asked a few of my older customers what they would do differently if they could turn back time. Some said, "I would've worried less!" Others, "I should've spent more time with my children!", or "I wish I had listened more, and lectured less!" Their sadness is based on the resulting damage they caused to their children. They finally understood how they could have helped their children reach for a healthier future; instead of driving them out. I also visit elders in nursing homes now and then. They are lonely and broken. They might interact with other residents, but most of them rarely have a visitor. Their mistakes cannot be undone. Life has passed them by already. The only sentence I hear over and over is, "I miss my family."

    I have so much compassion for them. Living with regrets sucks. Redemption is not up to them. Listening to them and praying over their unresolved issues is all one can offer. The rest is between them and God. If only I could help them forgive those who have disappointed them, and open themselves to God's grace. All things will be settled before Him some day. He won't judge us according to our deeds without weighing and measuring the intention of our hearts. That's why holding on to the past is dangerous to our souls. It causes us to harbor ill; whether we act on it or not.

    I wish I could view people's unsightly pasts through rose-colored glasses. If God forgives them; who am I to judge, right? I used to despise those who hurt innocent children and defenseless elders.   I wanted them to be hurt and beg for mercy.   My resentment and anger obviously intertwined with my own un-forgiveness.   I wouldn't let go of my mother's harsh methods of disciplining and controlling me.   That is why God delivered her to my care these days.   I am to forgive her!   God's grace enables me!   He tells me, "That which I won't let go is also holding me."   He wants me to detach myself from past offenses, so I can move forward.   And I don't want anything to paralyze my desire to live a better life; because I believe God has mighty plans for my future.   He's taught me to love my mother without having to like her.   He's able to judge the people He created.   He doesn't need my help.   These days, I feel sorry for those who harm others.   The lessons they're about to learn will bring them to their knees; until they feel shame and defeat.   And they will, some day, approach God with a willingness to make up for their actions.

How do I know I have forgiven my mother?   I no longer avoid her eyes.   I used to find criticism and disparagement in them during my formative years.   I was not able to look Mom straight in the face when we talked.   And that's why I chose to develop an entirely different relationship with my children.   I may have caused them embarrassment now and then; but they never endured the intentional digs and hateful remarks I had to live with.   All three of us communicate well for the most part.   I tell them everything; and I believe they do the same.   There is no fear of judgment among us.   We embrace it all.   We speak of each other's quirks as interesting, yet charming.   The idea of perfection doesn't intimidate us, as long as we're doing our best.

CHAPTER 7.   BUSINESS

Often suppressed by the negativity of this world, beauty is held within the soul.   Beauty waits patiently to be unleashed by the right purpose; so it'll never hide again.   Evil may delay its journey; but it can't destroy it.   We have no control over how life begins.   Nor do we know how and when it'll end.   But we can make it into an artful presentation by connecting the bits of information given to us.   We don't have to compete with others.   However, our beauty is just as unique and priceless as anyone else's.   Each one of us has creativity. It doesn't have to be about painting and sculpture.   It's more like an inner beauty and the appreciation of it.   We can also call it our spirituality or our immaterial reality.   It's centered within the deepest values by which we live.

The famous English poet and playwright William Shakespeare said, "Give me my robe, put on my crown; I have Immortal longings in me."   The gift of invention comes from God.   He is the inspiration behind it.   He gives us the courage to choose how best to display our inner beauty.   He encourages us to be bold with colors, words, or our hands.   Even a drab presentation is a form of art.   An insignificant wild flower in an open field is one of God's presentations.   If we take the time to notice one, we're taken aback by its breathtaking beauty. It's a display of innocence without the help of human intervention. What makes it more stunning is its surrounding.   It thrives regardless of extreme heat and aridity.   It may not have a huge impact on this complicated earth of ours; but a multitude of those tiny little flowers present the most amazing rug in the most unexpected places.   We don't stop to examine them one by one.   Yet they brighten our spirit while we're driving or walking through the nowhere world. The same is true about our few words of wisdom for people who pass through our lives. We have the capacity to enrich their psyche with joy and love.

Over the past decade, health professionals determined depression and chronic stress contribute to cardiovascular disease and diabetes. They discovered a tryst between creative arts and psychological health. They've proven how music, dance, visual arts, and expressive writing reduce the negative effects in life. Throughout history, we find people who use pictures, stories, dance, and chants as healing rituals.

My journey began twenty-five years ago when one of my customers' therapist told her he was going on a trip. She was panicking. She didn't think she could last a whole month without seeing him. He told her to write everything on a legal pad while he was away. "It'll serve the same purpose", he said; since he'd been doing a lot of the listening during their sessions. I thought that was a great advice. Something I could afford to do! My kids' father had left us while my business was still fresh. I too needed a lot of help. I needed someone other than my customers to listen to my pain. I certainly couldn't mix sadness and personal dilemma with my customers' time in my chair. It wouldn't be fair. So I decided to write every night. I wrote about six to ten pages each time. I poured out my anger and frustration onto those long yellow pages. At the beginning, I penciled hatred and vengeance for quite some time. Repetitions occurred. I wrote and rewrote the same events often. Eventually, I stopped dwelling over the past. I started expressing my present disappointments.   I wrote about someone's unfair behavior or their bad choice of words.   And some day, my daily six to ten page visits with my soul-filled notepads turned into Bible Studies and personal praise reports.   So healing did happen after all; leaving me with a passion for literary composition I never knew I had.

Art stems from imagination.   It's an expression; like choosing certain color clothes to wear in the morning that go well together. An artsy scarf serves as the finishing touch.   Abstract is art. Impressionism is art.   Even tattered clothes are considered a form of art.   Imagination is where emptiness roars and silence speaks.   It has a need to materialize.   We're the most satisfied when we're able to express ourselves.   And some experiences are hard to put into words. They're too painful.   We're way too limited when expressing grief; but our imagination can go the extra mile.   Some people turn to the arts to maintain or reconstruct their positive identity.

When asked "What would he do if he had a time machine," Sir Paul McCartney answered, "Go back and spend time with my mum." His mother Mary died at 47 from an embolism, following an operation for breast cancer, when young McCartney was only fourteen.   Her death had a lasting impact on him; which later helped him forge a strong bond with his Beatles' bandmate John Lennon, who too had lost his mother at a young age.   Julia Lennon was crossing the street when she got hit by a car driven by an off-duty police officer.   Though Julia had abandoned John at age five to be brought up by her sister Mimi, John was seventeen when he lost her a second time; but this was for good.   July 6, 1957 is considered one of the most important dates in music history.   It is when a fifteen-year-old Paul McCartney impressed a seventeen-year-old John Lennon with his rendition of Eddie Cochran's "Twenty Flight Rock". The two made a lifelong pact to continue their relationship and earnestly shook on it. This handshake was the only agreement they made. They never signed a written contract. Together they became the most beloved and successful songwriting team in the history of popular music, composing well over 200 unforgettable songs over a decade. Though they didn't publicize their common denominator; it was their grief that strengthened the bond between them.

True courage is standing out with joy and love in a world of bitterness and tragedy. It's about neutralizing the negative influences with a wave of euphoria; in other words, being contagious in a positive way. Conquering the bad with good. Soothing others with our gift, while we need the comforting the most. Unlike Himmler's perverted courage that consoled the SS soldiers during World War II as he said, "You are tough men willing to do the dirty work of war;" true courage is standing defiant, as one of the thousands of innocent Jews, and waiting to be murdered. Bravery shines when we're able to say: I want love and life to prevail, in spite of the adversary.

More people chase success thinking that will bring them comfort and money. Been there; done that! If we choose to be sincere and authentic, success will find us. We must be bold enough to question the things that don't rhyme with our heart. And we must never desire to be conformed to a world while questioning its immoral system. Our inner beauty gives us a sense of delight and wonder unlike anything else. It needs to be expressed on the outside of the person. People are impressed by what they see. Ministering to others anchors our faith; and we certainly don't need to shout about it. We can hold on to this amazing virtue and watch it transform those around us.   It is when this sacred inner architecture starts healing the uninspired, the unconnected, and the unappreciated that we are the most valuable to Divine works.   It is through the strength of our faith that we crawl and soar all at the same time.

     Today's people are way too comfortable.   They don't want to rock the boat.   They don't want to strain themselves.   More people seek therapy without a serious reason these days.   Any excuse will do!   It's those who are truly disturbed that need comfort and reassurance.   They need the encouragement.   We, as God's creative people, have the power to inspire the society we live in.   We can spur motivation with a smile.   We can bring down the walls of fear and insecurity.   The world, with its decay, is changeable.   In fact, it's being changed every day through media and advertisement.   People who are in charge of all that may as well sit back and have a good laugh.   They are constantly rearranging to refresh the message!

     One of our biggest mistakes is that we don't stop to listen without judgment.   When we hear the sordid details of someone's life, we judge him without mercy.   If we could only make ourselves available to listen without passing judgments, we may understand their circumstances better.   Everyone's journey is unique.   Everyone's values are different.   That's why life is so interesting.   Sometimes lending an ear is the only gift people need in order to get to the root of their problem.   Compassion is a far better vessel than judgment.   It turns our faces to better horizons.

Being judgmental of others is about *us*. It has very little to do with them. The day we accept others, just as they are, is the day we accept ourselves, just as we are. It's a form of forgiving ourselves. Sigmund Freud's theory about psychological projection is well-established in contemporary psychology. It explains the defense mechanism whereby we project our undesirable thoughts, motivations, desires, and feelings onto others. The mind is a complex mechanism. It holds too much information; making a jumbled mess. By letting go of the past, we release our resistance to the flow of today's life, as well as to its flow of good circumstances. We're constantly shaping, reinventing, and writing our own story. We're not where we'd like to be. But that doesn't mean we shouldn't enjoy the present!

Beauty is invoked within a field of wild flowers, in the smell of a good cup of coffee, or on the tattered pages of an old book. We know how to discover it. When we breathe in air, we can envision it flowing through our diaphragm, and filling our lungs. We can hold it in for a little bit; and let it out, while being thankful for such a gift we take for granted. Some of our brothers and sisters suffer from asthma, with their airways being inflamed all the time. They live with a painful tightness in the chest. Coughing and wheezing are their lifelong companions. This simple task of breathing in and out is painful. Compassion towards the sufferers around us can lead us to an eagerness to be mindful of the beauty and the harmony we find in each day. We must allow our minds to be transformed. An attitude of gratitude can do that.

Rocambole was a fictional character dreamed up by the French writer Pierre Alexis Ponson du Terrail during the 19th century. Rocambole, is a resourceful orphan who ends up on the wrong side of the law. He was an adventurer and a criminal who redeemed himself, and devoted his life to good.   The character's success provided good income to Ponson du Terrail, who continued churning out his adventures.   In total, he wrote nine Rocambole novels. Around 1870, as Ponson de Terrail embarked on a new Rocambole saga, Emperor Napoleon III surrendered to Germany.   At the time Ponson fled Paris, he gathered like-minded companions and together they formed a guerilla warrior force until the Germans burned down his castle.   A role reversal took.   Imagination is an ultimate power. It cannot be underestimated.   The key to turning imagination into reality is to live in the imagined scene!   Reality conforms to our wish! What we believe, we become.   The fictional Rocambole, penned by Ponson du Terrail, lived his author's dreams.   Ponson died in 1871, leaving the saga of Rocambole incomplete.   He was forty-two; the same age as Rocambole.

  Ponson lived his life as he envisioned it; leaving behind great literature and the word "rocambolesque".   In French it describes any fantastic adventure, especially those with twists and turns in the story. Ponson du Terrail's life may have been short; but it produced a legacy. He did what he was here to do.   Too many people go to their grave with their gift to the world ungiven.   They're too afraid to unwrap it, or too afraid of to fail.   Remember, life is the most amazing gift we'll ever receive.   It must be experienced fully!

  The views of each person are important.   We lower our standards if we don't say what we mean; especially if we are trying to spare others' feelings, or seek their approval.   This stunts our own growth.   First and foremost, we must be true to ourselves.   It certainly is important to respect and encourage those around us.   And we can and should motivate them every chance we get.   But we shouldn't shortchange ourselves either.   How we think, feel, and act during our challenges determines the difference between hope and despair, optimism and frustration, victory and defeat.   We must never let our tribulations weaken our faith.   Faith is our only anchor.   It holds us against the tides of life.   It heals our wounds.   It allows us to breathe and rest during our frustrations.   It'll never let us down.   And it can't be taught.   So we must hold on to what we have.   It cannot be replaced or substituted.

God didn't place us in this world to be passive sojourners.   There are times in our lives when passivity is necessary.   It helps us catch our breath after a huge ordeal.   This is understandable and commendable.   But when we make passivity a lifestyle; we're not living up to God's expectations.   The willingness to accept our lives doesn't mean we sacrifice our preferences and needs in order to help others meet their preferences and needs.   We must never let go of our goals and objectives for the sake of becoming a hero for someone else.   I'm an expert on unnecessary sacrifices and wasted efforts for people who didn't care about me.   They simply demanded more.   And I went along because I needed to earn their approval.   Do I have the right to resent them?   I don't think so.   They were the rejects and the misfits; just like I was to a certain extent.

Being a hairdresser wasn't an option for women in Istanbul when I was growing up.   Hairdressers were men, walking around with color-stained hands. They didn't wear gloves. Women in the industry gave manicures and pedicures in those days. Becoming a hairdresser was never my dream. Yet I've been standing behind the chair for over three decades. I enjoy what I do. It's gratifying. My main focus is about delivering the changes my customers want and I try to please them. I love seeing a smile as they are handing me back the mirror. I've learned to disassociate myself from my performance. I try not to have hurt feelings if someone isn't satisfied with my work. There's always room for improvement. And by the same token, I try not to get a big head when I receive their praise. I thank God for that.

Recent studies reveal connections between cosmetic surgery and psychiatry. In fact, the aesthetic alteration of facial features can bring an uplift in attitude and an improvement in outlook. I can heal the dissatisfaction within. Dermatology and plastic surgery can be important especially to teenagers; because they might aid their cognitive development. Many believe undergoing physical change increases overall quality of life. And it does! A positive image equips people to enjoy a better quality of life.

The beauty field is not complicated. Our results are not earth shattering. What we cherish the most is when customers share their story. The depth of it grows with each visit. We love their camaraderie just as much as they love their improving appearance. Some customers start interacting without even knowing why they should trust us. But one way or the other, that heart-to-heart is hard to resist. We learn from one another. We exchange encouraging words. Together, we bring up the beauty within and weed out the negativity. It would be fair to describe my profession as, "A reality of creating illusion."

     Obviously, we don't leave them in an unflattering look. We improve hair and skin as we go along. When hair feels good again, we come up with a new improvement. We color. We curl. Then we recommend products that could make it look and feel natural. We're full of new and creative ideas. Our greatest accomplishment happens when we take total strangers and upgrade them into lasting relationships. Honesty, trust, and respect take us to deeper levels of connectedness. They create lasting connections; where we value each other's space and personality, without expecting anything else. Lending a compassionate ear makes all the difference. Once connected, it's hard to say goodbye. Everyone matters. We hope they feel the same about us, and wait patiently to hear from them again.

     My success in the beauty industry comes from listening to people's suggestions or criticisms. I take them very seriously. Some of those may not be a possibility to accomplish; but being sincere with those who take the time to help me improve is vital. Things constantly change in the world. Today's customer has a high standard. They're knowledgeable, and they want the best. Transparency is the only way to win their loyalty. And sometimes I've been blessed to win their faith in me as well. There is a difference between the two. Loyalty is a commitment based on one's experience. It's an intellectual and practical choice. However, faithfulness involves the heart. It produces a passion-infused dedication for the future. And only a handful will risk the future.

I think of the time when my last boss stopped by for five minutes to announce he was closing the business by the end of the month. We had less than three weeks to vacate and find a decent salon for our customers. I was devastated. I cried in frustration. It felt so unfair! I loved my work environment. It was the best salon in the area. I remember saying, "I wish I owned my own place so nobody can decide on my behalf." Dad asked, "Do you believe you can run a business?" "Yep!" I replied. And the rest is history.

One of my customers who worked as a rental agent for a commercial property took me to a small business location. It had fresh paint and carpeting. The previous tenants had closed their business within a short time. The landlord offered me a good rate if I were to take over "as is." That's all I could afford to do anyway. The only problem was the fact that the property was divided into private rooms; since it used to be a money lending business. I decided it couldn't hurt; since I only had one other stylist courageous enough to join me. Within three weeks, Dad's arduous engineering and craftsmanship produced a couple of stations for us. The day I opened the doors for business was when my "business license" arrived in the mail; along with the eighteen-wheeler that delivered the hydraulic chairs for the stations and the shampoo area. I only had a few products on the shelves. Yet by the time my first customer was getting ready to pay me, two other customers walked in! They were wanting to make a purchase so they could give me my first "dollar". I received from all three at the same time. I could never forget their faithfulness. In fact, all three are still with me; and they continue to believe in me. And I thank God every day for those who believe in me more than I believe in myself.

This is, without a doubt, a faith-based business. I walk in every morning and pray over everyone with whom we will come in contact during the day. I ask God to help us be the best that we can be. I don't believe we are so great that we don't need God's help. People's needs are multifaceted. Some crave to be heard. They need to be validated. Others are trying to fight physical or emotional challenges. Perhaps the only thing they can change that day is their hairstyle. We, as hairdressers, can be the stepping stone for those who are off balance for unexpected reasons. We play a temporary, but a positive role. The customers leave feeling uplifted and beautiful. It is during those times that we're more than "just a hairdresser".

Challenges come unannounced and uninvited. They catch us by surprise. They take our breath away. They cause confusion. They may even cause us to derail occasionally. But they can also produce perseverance, determination, courage, optimism, trust, and faith; none of which grows without challenges. Sir Charles Spencer, "Charlie" Chaplin (1889 - 1977) was an English comic actor, filmmaker, and composer who rose to fame in the silent era. He is one of the most important figures in the history of film. His childhood in London was one of poverty and hardship. As a single parent, his mother struggled. She was forced to take stage jobs in small theaters to feed her children. She pawned her stage gowns to pay the rent. Her faltering career came to a halt one night when her singing voice cracked and sank to a whisper in the middle of her act; and the audience cruelly laughed her off the stage. Charlie was listening in the wings, appalled by his mother's humiliation. Already a talented mimic, he took his mother's place in the spotlight and finished her act.

He was five years old!   Young Chaplin struggled to keep up with his mother's physical and emotional needs until she had to go to an asylum.   Though he suffered many setbacks - often booed off stage, just as his mother had been – Charlie finally landed a lucrative contract that earned him a ticket to America.   At age twenty-one, confident in his future, Charlie Chaplin arrived at the docks in Manhattan.   He took his hat off and shouted, "America, I'm coming to conquer you!   Every man, woman and child shall have my name on their lips - Charles Spencer Chaplin!"   He was right!   He knew his famous persona "the Little Tramp" intimately.   He explained, "He was myself, a comic spirit within me that said 'I must express myself' ".

Challenges come to us all.   How we respond to them makes all the difference.   They become our greatest friends when we treat each challenge as a stepping stone.   The way we handle them determines its outcome.   Winston Churchill said, "Success consists of going from failure to failure, without loss of enthusiasm."   He is right.   There are no losers in life; only those who give up on themselves.   Having deep faith in *who* we are, regardless of what others may think, is the key to our hidden treasure.   This belief in ourselves is so priceless that those who try to put us down will end up saluting our triumphs someday.   So we must keep going out on the limb, even if we are afraid it might break.   We are bound to reach the succulent fruit at its end!   The magic potion isn't our perseverance or our bullheadedness.   It is our faith!

Living out our dreams begins when we start walking in the right direction.   The information needed for the journey is never there from the beginning.   If it were, how are we to develop faith?

The vital pieces of information we need start coming our way as we're trudging up the mountain, tired and discouraged, almost ready to give up. Those encouraging details find us when we least expect them. Hanging by a thread may sound disorienting; but it's a figure of speech. It means we scrabble up the mountain, hoping to reach the top. Hope might seem a bit flimsy at that point.   But hope is more than that.   It's a lasso coiled tightly around our torso that will never break, so long as we allow God to hold us.   A God who has the life-giving power to bring all things into existence, without the use of any preexisting substance, is not about to let us slip through His powerful grip.   In fact, it is during those times that we're closer to Him than we have ever been.

      Like I said before, becoming a hairdresser was never my dream.   I started as a shampoo-girl in a salon so I could be around other people.   I didn't speak English at the time.   That's all I qualified for.   But I was grateful for the position; because I didn't have to communicate.   And I earned twenty-five cents per shampoo.   Iris was with me for about three months, until I knew I could afford a daycare for her.   She needed to interact with other children.   Once I enrolled her in a reputable day school, I felt confident that she had a chance to a part of this new country.   I was the happiest shampoo-girl from then on.   When the nail technician walked out unannounced, leaving behind many disappointed customers, I jumped on the opportunity.   I didn't need to chat while I worked on their hands; and they already knew me.   So I became the happiest manicurist in town. The only time I resisted was when my boss offered me an apprenticeship to become a hairdresser.   This one involved my going to school at night.   I was already sad that I couldn't be there when my kids came home in from school.   So I turned down his offer.   And I turned it down a second time.   The third time made me mad.   I said, "Oh...okay!", with an attitude.   Little did I know then how much our future was going to depend on that one decision.   The kids' father and I divorced shortly after; and my new profession became quite the provider for decades.

CHAPTER 8.   FORGIVENESS

I walked into Iris's bedroom one day and found her crying. She might have been twelve or thirteen at the time. I reacted poorly. I was being insensitive and obnoxious. After a quick tantrum, I stormed out of her room; slamming the door. I took several steps down the stairs and stopped. I hadn't even asked her why she was crying. I hated myself for doing that. My mother had never allowed tears when we were growing up. And I had become her. I ran upstairs into Iris' bedroom again. As soon as she saw me walk in, she wiped away her tears. I felt terrible. I hugged her and started crying. I asked her to please forgive me. My mother's bad habit could not excuse my behavior. Once we both calmed down, I listened to what had caused her the pain. I can't remember the context of our conversation, but I will never forget the shame I carried from then on that reminded me how easy it was to become the person I disliked the most.

I admit; I wanted to be *liked* by my mother for the longest time; even though I didn't want to be like her. That sounds irrational now. Her constant disapproval of me created my judgment of her. Carl Jung said, "Everything that irritates us about others can lead us to a better understanding of ourselves." That's so irritating! At first glance, it makes me think that I must not have understood myself at all; since I disliked Mom for so many reasons. But there is more to it. It also tells me that, if I dislike a person, I might be disapproving of myself to a certain extent. I need the courage to discern what I dislike about myself; before it all turns into an endless combat.

Pointing a finger at others' flaws is senseless; especially when they don't believe there's anything wrong with them. That's why I should work on my own instead; while I still can. Naturally, it's hard to shed light on one's own negative traits. That's probably why I had been concentrating on Mom's problems all that time. But when I saw that I was causing my own child the kind of pain I had endured, it was time to face myself! I was going to set a better example for her to follow. Children imitate us more than we think. My goal was to become a beacon of laughter, resolution, and grace; none of which was possible without a genuine forgiveness toward my mother.

That was a huge awakening for me! Until that day, I had never realized that I could be like Mom. That was the first day I became aware of it. It was humbling. The nature of God's judgment is based on how forgiving we are. If we want to be close to Him, we must practice His Way: joy, love, and forgiveness. When we fail to treat one another as God treats us, we separate ourselves from His lovingkindness. I remember this older lady who sat in my chair. I had never seen her before. She was given a gift certificate by someone I knew. When I started cutting her hair is when she began to cry. It was late; and I was too tired to minister to her at the time. She kept saying, "I don't want to talk about this anymore! I'm sick and tired of it!" After watching her struggle for a while, I understood that I was expected to listen to what troubled her so deeply. So I said, "Obviously, there's something I'm supposed to hear from you; and perhaps, you are supposed to hear something from me." Then she told me how her father, a pastor of a huge church, molested her and her little sister as young girls. She hadn't understood why God allowed this awful man's ministry to grow; regardless of his terrible sin.

I asked her, "Are you trying to judge God's righteousness?" She said, "Absolutely not!" I told her that someday she would be standing before the Almighty and asking for forgiveness, when she hadn't forgiven her own father. The measure we use to give out for others is the measure God uses for us. I told her that God's judgment is flawless; and in due time, her father too will stand before God, giving account for his own trespasses. Never to doubt God! He gives and He takes away! Then, she confessed: "I've been going from one therapist to another for years. No one ever told me that I had been doubting God's righteousness with my ongoing questions." Revelation cannot be forced upon people. They have to be ripe and ready for it. That day was a divine appointment. Neither one of us wanted to talk; yet a great result took place because of our obedience.

We can ask God all sorts of questions; but we should never question His righteousness. It was easy for me to tell this lady how she had been wrong to judge and hold resentment against her father. But through her, I was also given a chance to see myself the way God saw me. I was embarrassed; because I had been harboring the same feelings toward my own mother. Let's just say, we both learned a valuable lesson at the same time. It's easy to judge others for their deeds, while we judge ourselves for our intentions. But *judging* is wrong with or without a motive. As we fuse more and more with our judgments, we perceive different realities. And the more we continue this pattern, the darker our reality becomes. What are we supposed to do when the person we have been begrudging might end up reconnecting with God someday and decide to take on his redemptive walk? Are we going to tell God not to forgive him, because we haven't been able to do so? God broke me that day;

because I had been breaking His heart for quite some time. People might break us over and over again. But when God breaks us, something awesome takes place.

A broken soul is like an alabaster box that contains expensive perfume. Its sweet aroma rises to heaven. God recognizes it. How could He not? It belongs to Him. Its fragrance signals our troubled spirit. It's a composition of our failure, defeat, and frustration. It's our special pass to God's help; through which He teaches us humility, patience, and hope. He receives us with open arms and embraces our weakness. He kisses and soothes our pain. He empowers us with His everlasting strength. He eliminates our agony and all of its effects. He grants us victories as we follow His Divine Map. His wisdom sheds light unto our path; demolishing all of our unnecessary obstacles!

Gary Leon Ridgway, commonly known as the Green River Killer, confessed in 2003 to killing thirty-eight women. At his sentencing, the families of his victims had the opportunity to speak out to him. They expressed unimaginable grief and anger toward him. When the time came for Robert Rule, the father of teenage victim Linda Jane Rule, to speak, he told Ridgway: "Mr. Ridgway, there are people here that hate you. I am not one of them. You have made it difficult to do what I believe, which is what God says to do, and that is to forgive. You are forgiven, Sir." Ridgway who sat emotionless the entire time, teared up after those words.

God's justice is His promise to us. He doesn't need our help. If we want Him to take over our pain and suffering, we must first release them to Him.   And the only way to let go is through forgiveness.   Believe me, if forgiveness wasn't an important attribute for us to develop, He would not have spoken the following words at the moment of his earthly death: "Father, forgive them for they know not what they do."   He would have zapped His abusers and be done with it.   But He didn't.   Instead, He prayed for them.   He still doesn't like seeing us hurt.   In order for us to see the ultimate justice, there must be forgiveness.   Pardoning someone doesn't take away the consequences for their actions.   Everyone pays for his deeds.   But the consequences of un-forgiveness will harm our soul!   Un-forgiveness is like cancer.   It'll eat us from the inside out.   It'll weaken our foundation.   Forgiveness is an act of strength.   It's the gift that keeps giving.   It's the peace of mind that calms even the deadliest tempest.   It'll give us wings to fly and the transparency to see which way we're going.   It's a permission slip for a fuller and a happier life!

  God isn't impressed with our address, occupation, or social role.   He allows us to control the day to day happenings in our lives.   He cares not what part we play, as long as we play it well.   He wants our attitude to line up with His; regardless of our circumstances.   And if it doesn't, He'll make the proper adjustments to fit us right in.   Our strengths are gifts from God.   He gives them so we may help ourselves and others.   He will support us in our weakness.   And if we desire, He will use us to help others.   Moses' speech becomes a powerful warning to his enemy, the Pharaoh.   Rahab's wretched existence is given a different purpose as she schemes against her own people who have oppressed her.   Peter's bitter tears as he denied Jesus three times became his conviction as the leader of the Apostles.

Our soul's capacity needs to be plowed every so often; because God expects us to produce a better harvest.   He stretches us until we master growth.   A broken soul is not the end of goodness and beauty; it's actually the most perfect soil for goodness and beauty to grow.

    Our lives are designed to be the vessels of God's grace and victory.   He loves it when we're joy-filled and triumphant.   He pours His light into us.   His spirit uplifts this shallow and hardened world through us.   He shows us off as His true children.   Our unique melody might help others to remember their own tunes.   Through us, they might see God's covenant blessings are real.   Our lifestyle will impress them sooner or later.   Our positive outlook on life might even inspire them to pick up their own broken instruments and start harmonizing.   They will remember their God-given composition someday.   Their musically inclined ears will acknowledge and welcome His notes.

    C. S. Lewis, the well-known author of The Chronicles of Narnia as well as a slew of Christian essays and novels, was born in Ireland in 1898.   He grew up in a church-going family; but became an atheist at age 15, when he started to view his religion as a chore and a duty.   He was bothered by evil and suffering in the world that didn't fit with the God he imagined.   Though he was reluctant to take in religion itself, through Christianity, Lewis found a satisfactory explanation: "Suffering and pain have purpose."   In 1931, following a long discussion and late-night walk with his close friend J.R.R Tolkien, he committed to the Christian belief.   His faith changed his direction from "self-scrutiny" to "self-forgetfulness".   He became an ardent defender of Christian faith saying, "Only the unsophisticated could mistake the Christian myth for history."

Faith is seeing things from God's perspective. It's a privilege. It's something to celebrate. It helps us waltz through life. And God's greatest pleasure is to see us dance passionately; especially during our brokenness. He wants us to make our own instruments and play our own tunes. The bumps in the road, disillusionments, and disappointments might slow us down. But they definitely add expression to our tempo. The beat of our songs display how deeply we rely on God. The worry-free moves of our spirit reflect our appreciation of Him. Our heart flutters as our music puts a smile on His face. God sees our love for Him in lieu of our iniquities; as He loves us in spite of ourselves.

Discovering God's love for me is the greatest success of my life. He is my personal pamphlet I have reread a million times. In it, He describes everything about me. His words of encouragement inspire me. Each sentence brings me closer; as each paragraph shapes our relationship. Every chapter explains who I am. And through Him, I find a deeper and a more valuable *me*. We are inseparable at this point! He fills me with peace and satisfaction. He refuels me with fresh energy and excitement. With Him by my side, challenge cannot exhaust me.

My good friend Garrett worked for me for a decade. I believe he needed my help. He had started drinking as a young teenager; and gotten progressively worse. He continued to disappoint many of his customers by calling in sick quite frequently. I started doing his chores, so I could keep him on the payroll. I wanted him to walk away from his addiction. Looking after him became a chore. It was exhausting. But I never gave up; until one day, I heard David Jeremiah on the radio say, "People don't get saved because of our perseverance; they get saved because of the Holy Spirit." I made a difficult decision that morning. I terminated Garrett's position saying, "I've been standing in your way all this time. You have been determined to go places I'm no longer willing to go with you." He was sad and highly surprised. I was shocked! But I wasn't trying to give up on him. I was being obedient. And I knew it was the right thing to do.

God had sprinkled wisdom upon me as I traveled to work that morning. He gave clarity to my foggy thoughts. He wiped away the blur. The God of Abraham, Isaac, and Jacob; the only Living God; freed me from that unnecessary burden. I believe that message ministered to me in several ways that day. It redesigned my path. It helped me understand my relationship with Mom as well. I had been mad at myself for not being able to get along with her. I had listened to customers and friends who loved their mothers. And those who had lost their mothers spoke of how they miss them all the time. I didn't think I would ever miss mine. I felt like I was a thorn in her side. We didn't just have occasional disagreements. We never agreed on anything! If I said white; she said black. There was a spirit of discontentment between us that needed the help of the Holy Spirit. I prayed that God would help us both, and turned the situation over to Him. I had to free myself from that extra pressure.

I still watch her be miserable over the slightest little detail. She is eighty-one years old. Now that she understands more about God; she believes God is trying to instill *patience* into her. I asked her one day, "You must be waiting for something if you believe it's challenging your patience. What are you missing?" She thought for a while. She didn't really have an answer. All she knew was that she was unhappy. But she didn't know why. Being her only caregiver after Dad's death, I have been walking in his shoes for more than nine years. And I often wonder how he kept his sanity. I'm not trying to keep her happy. That's a full time job. My sense of accomplishment is no longer at Mom's mercy.

    I believe Istanbul set the stage for my Mom's fears and insecurities. It had already devoured her way before I stepped into the picture. Pessimism had molded her into a negative, bitter, and unforgiving woman who murmured and complained about everything. She seasoned my life with negativity. I accepted her follies and superstitions. Sneezing once meant something different than sneezing twice. And sneezing as you're walking out the door was awful. That meant bad luck to the nth degree. An extra place setting meant a stranger would come to dinner. Laughing out loud was improper. Who knows what that was about!? A bad situation was due to a previous sin. It was a punishment for what I must've done. Considering the long list of sins we all could fall into, God must have been cruel. Mom's view of God was a mix between a superpower and a superstition. He was a hair-raising, spine-chilling, blood-curdling character. He kept a chart of my deeds. He wanted me to fail. He was eager to put me in my place. I had to outsmart this god-monster. My young and innocent brain found a solution. If I walked on a straight-as-an-arrow kind of path, God couldn't find anything to punish me for. And if I sprinkled a good deed now and then, He would leave me alone. I would be on His list of "good people".

That belief is a mistake people learn the hard way. Believing we will earn God's love and approval with good deeds is false. He already loves us no matter what. Because He loves us as a Father, He desires to teach us the *holiness* we need to enjoy a relationship with Him, right here and right now. We don't need to wait until we get to heaven. We can be one with God while in this world. Holiness comes through simple heavenly ethics: Love God with all your heart and all your mind, and love your neighbor as yourself. We must make room for these simple commands. They can replace the angst and the yearning for the wrong things due to our flawed upbringing. Forgiveness revokes anger and hatred. Contentment annuls greed and covetousness. Thankfulness overrides complaints and grumbling. Those qualities lead to inner peace; but they require an intense effort to seep through all of the adversities with whom we are surrounded. Our human nature resists them as well. So we must desire them enough to drag them in, and be determined to fight for them during our challenging times. We did possess all of those in the Garden of Eden. But today, we must make a vigorous and determined attempt to regain them.

Though both my parents possessed some idea of God; neither one told me about His endless love for me. They weren't trying to keep me from knowing God. They simply didn't know Him well. They were immersed in a shame and guilt-ridden world. God and I were never introduced the right way. His awesome presence was muddied with unkind depictions. So He used my humiliation to initiate a relationship with me. Each pain became a step in the right direction. It was my staircase to heaven. Once I gave myself to Him completely, God bathed me with His grace. He pursued, upheld, and sanctified me while my belief in Him became my only reality.   This Ancient Being who created the earth and everything in it, became my Father.   Thunder and lightning didn't express His anger.   Earthquakes and famines were not His way of sifting humanity.   I'd been afraid of Him for all the wrong reasons.

God re-entered my life in small portions; and He never left.   He saw my anguish and He could tell I didn't have enough air to breathe in during my fearful times.   His breath penetrated me through Dad's encouraging words.   They chased away all of my doubts, one by one.   They sprinkled "hope" and sowed "patience" into me.   They gave me the motivation to be a better person.   They helped me see myself more clearly.

God wasn't going to let me drown.   He gave me Dad's humor as a float.   I latched on to it.   With my frail arms tightly wrapped for safety, God carried me in His arms.   I remember the victories of our buoyancy together.   God was the intense light I was drawn to through Dad's sweet presence.   He liberated me from fears and insecurities.   They used to be a huge burden at my young age.   He healed my heart piece by piece, as He took up residence in me.   And through Dad's example of leadership, I found the "strength" to imagine a better future for myself.

Through Jirayr's birth, God gave me my first "responsibility".   I was to take care of this little person.   I was to look after him.   I had to be a good role model!   I wanted to walk as straight as possible so Jirayr could follow my steps.   I entertained him with fun games.   I showered him with positive ideas and stories.   In that sense, I became Dad's little helper. I tried to play a good part in a world of bad examples. His innocence was priceless. I couldn't stand to see him hurt. Even though Mom treated him differently, I still didn't want to take a chance. I guarded him. The love that I had received from Dad grew deeper through Jirayr. It blossomed into a sacrificial level.

Then I tasted God's unconditional "love" through my kids, Iris and Osheen. Those two precious lives were bestowed on me. I was honored to be a parent. God must have really loved me to give me such huge blessings. His love took deeper roots in my heart. And it continued to grow until He was the Parent one day. God's parenting was awe-inspiring. I had to let Him lead. So God became the head of our household. I prayed. I begged. I pleaded for Him to make me a better listener. He opened the doors to His heavenly supplies and poured abundance. He kept us safe and healthy. He gave us wisdom. Our mistakes were easy to undo. Single parenting was a breeze with God. He helped us get past the challenges of a broken family. Our lacks didn't cripple us. In fact, I even received occasional praises for being a good mom when I owed it all to God. As I trusted Him with everything, He made me the star! God transformed me!

God was the "compassion" I learned through humility. It kept growing until it possessed me entirely. I dropped my judgmental and discriminating thoughts. I saw people as my equal. I saw beyond their inabilities. I walked through their difficulties with them. I became the staff they could hold on to. I felt their pain, cried, and offered intercessory prayers over their hurts. I refused to grow tired.

I didn't quit. I waited until they could stand tall, and be able to walk alone. Their success wasn't my testimony; so I never talked about it. It belonged to God. He was to be praised. I believed if He could use me, He could use anyone. My gratitude is always overflowing. That's how happy and content I am!

God is the "courage" I found on the streets of parenthood. I needed it when I opened a business. I could barely speak English at the time. God minimized my mistakes, so I could overcome the damages. When someone tampered with my stability whether it be physical, mental, or emotional, God helped me recognize their motives. He gave me the wisdom to handle their evil choices. I didn't need to roar. I didn't even have to fight back. God simply took them out of my life. He put them where they belong. He was the unwavering shield that protected me against stabbings like, "Our gathering won't be perfect until you join us with a husband;" or "Our table will not be complete until you have a man sitting next to you." Such criticisms were intended to make me feel low. They were to cause pain and darkness every time I heard them. Yet God's light extinguished all of their effects. I saw my way around just enough to take baby-steps. I focused only on what needed to be done each day. I had already admitted my incompetence as a single mother. There was no shame in it. Proverbs 11: 2 reads, "Pride leads to disgrace; but with humility comes wisdom." Our success depends on getting rid of pride. Otherwise it blinds us. It breeds arrogance; as we reject corrections. It slowly gnaws away at our bounty until we're destroyed, disgraced, and shamed. So it's better to start with shame; and do it willingly so we can improve.

Understanding and accepting the presence of a Good God was more than satisfying. It was life-giving. God didn't enjoy punishing me. He didn't even want to punish me. My wrong actions punished me! God preferred rewarding me instead. His unfailing love slowly opened the eyes of my heart. My worth was determined by the Creator of this world and the world to come. I realized God adored me just as I adore my brother and my children. God waited for me to approach Him. He didn't mind it if I asked for a favor! He expected me to! God was always willing and ready to grant my needs. None of His promises came with a price! I didn't have to earn any of them. He lavished everything on me because I belonged to Him. Giving God the reins of my life was the smartest thing I have ever done. I now see my future through His eyes. I desire to operate through His abilities. And I'm glad God didn't allow me more knowledge than I could handle. He spoon-fed me one truth at a time, with each experience; as He saw fit. The abundance I received by following His lead is mind-boggling.

Starting life with an awesome dad was rewarding. The importance of belonging took shape with Dad and eventually transformed into a bigger need. That's why surrendering to God was easy for me. He was to be in charge of my life. He was to help me make good choices. He was to lay out better opportunities. His love was comforting. I welcomed His peace! I'm sad for those who don't know they have the same privilege. If only they could see how easy life becomes once they stop battling their own weaknesses.

Today, I have Mom under my wing. I care for her. I see to it that her needs are met. I don't forget our past. Yet I believe we have a better future. She has accepted God's love as her potion for healing. We still have many differences; but they're not debilitating. Actually, we're more in synch now than we've ever been. She's gentler and kinder. She's fun to be around. I enjoy her company. I thank God for allowing me a fresh start with her. I'm so glad I got to know her. She has never apologized for any of her mistakes; and most likely, she never will. The way I tend her these days is meant to correct her; and also to demonstrate what we should've been like in the past. It helps me with all of my disappointments. Not everyone will ask for our forgiveness; but we're expected to grant it to each person. This heightened level of understanding comes when we truly grasp God's forgiveness. He gave his life to prove it to us! There's nothing more humbling than that!

I've been back to Istanbul several times. I've made peace with it. I forgave all of its idiosyncrasies. Today's Istanbul may be one of the safest large cities in the world. It may have a lower crime rate than London, Paris, and Berlin. Its famous hospitality is recognized worldwide. Its men and women can work and socialize together. Religion is a less volatile issue, since the majority of its non-Muslim population has already fled. I don't go to Istanbul to observe its culture. Nor do I care to see its improvements. I go because of my family. And I'm not concerned about crime or violence. Those are prevalent all over the world. Greed is everywhere. And it'll only get worse if we walk away from God's standards of Peace and Forgiveness!

Our weakest hour is also our finest. God reveals Himself in our emotional transparency. The mountaintop experiences give us only an illusion of Him.   But if we long for a relationship with Him, we must also learn to embrace humility and peace.   Losing our wealth, status, or level of comfort shouldn't destroy us.   We can rise above all of our brokenness; which is what gets His attention.   God doesn't work through those who think they're all together.   He doesn't need any of their strengths.   He only desires to use those who admit their imperfections.   Our ego must die before we're spiritually healthy again.   God's reflection in a puddle of our tears is the most perfect display of His presence.   It stays with us forever.

CHAPTER 9. CONCLUSION

Iris and I went to see the movie "Finding Nemo" in the theater one Saturday evening. She was twenty-five at the time. The movie portrays a daddy clown fish looking for his abducted son, Nemo. It is a fascinating story about yearning, determination, and endurance in the name of love. While Nemo was a captive in a fish tank at a dentist's office; his father, Marlin, traveled great distance and encountered dangerous sea creatures to find him. And Nemo came up with a couple of escape ideas of his own. At the end, they reunite and return home. Nemo goes off to school and his Dad is no longer overprotective, proudly watching him swim away. The writer and director of this beautiful animated feature, Andrew Stanton, loved going to his dentist's office as a child where he admired the fish tank. He assumed the fish were from the ocean and would want to go home. That's what inspired him to write Nemo's story. It is touching and exhilarating all at the same time.

When we walked out of the theater that night, Iris' eyelids were swollen; and her eyes red and puffy from crying. The story had a sad twist; but it didn't affect me like it did Iris. She didn't want to talk about it. So I didn't insist. But I pondered. I knew Iris grieved over her father leaving; even though she and I never discussed it before. I thought she had been protecting me over the years by not bringing up the subject. And I certainly didn't want to intrude; thinking she'll talk when she's ready. She emptied herself during the entire movie, as if her own tank came apart. It was her time to grieve over the unrealized portion of her father-and-daughter dream. But a decade later, her dad did walk her down the aisle, and her script ended up writing her a happy ending.

I think of that film now and then. I wonder if Mr. Stanton - working on the story of his own healing - knew he would be helping Iris with her own closure some day? I wondered when my turn would come. What would it take to empty my cache of tears? Was it still a bucketful? Or had it turned into a well by now? What if I ended up falling into my own well? My unrealized hopes deserved a proper burial as well; if I wanted a safe journey to wholeness. When would I be ready for it? I'm fifty-nine years old already. I've stopped asking, "Where did I go wrong?" or "How could I have done it differently?" Those questions no longer haunt me. In the past, every time I managed to take a few steps in the right direction, the unlived segments of my life demanded some kind of validation. I either fought the urge tooth and nail; or ended up attracting the next bully.

My moment of grief never came. I never took the time to mourn over what it would've been like. Will I get there later; or has it already happened? Will I ever hear an apology? I don't think so; but it sure sounds good. I'm also entertaining the idea of apologizing to my mother someday – like opening the door. The Bible says: "Give, and it will be given to you. A good measure, pressed down, shaken together, and flowing over, will be poured upon your lap. The measure you use will be the measure you receive." I haven't made it that far. Still thinking about it!

The most intense of all human interactions is a sincere apology! Because this particular interaction requires "humility" on one side and "acceptance" on the other; both necessary for healing, regardless of how deep the wound. If heartfelt, an apology is strong enough to uproot anger, bitterness, and grudges instantly. The benefits are unlimited as they set everyone free! In some cases, forgiveness is a transaction. It comes as a result of an apology. But there are times when it's internal. If our offender is no longer with us; because of death or other form of departure, we can accept his apology in the spirit. Holding people responsible for things they can't undo is futile. It requires our grace to cancel the debt. And human grace is found in forgiveness! Humility and Grace forge meaningful relationships.

One way to explore human nature is by admitting that opposites exist. Evil does exist. The evidence is loud and clear. There's a widespread suffering around us; and sometimes within us. That's the part of our nature we should not dwell on. Wrong ideas and actions surface quickly, leaving bitterness and sorrow behind. Evil is rampant; and God wants us to resist it. He allows us to fail; and He helps us if and when we ask. He walks with us as we make our way here on Earth. And as we rely on Him for strength and endurance; God brings forth our best fruits. The journey of Faith is not about sitting back and letting God win our victories. It's about leaning on Him until our spirit is filled with steadfastness, stamina, and tenacity. Our perseverance comes from our desire to pursue a goal that's beyond our earthly life; and to strengthen the ability to deal with setbacks and failures along the way. It involves keeping our eyes on the prize; while doing the right thing all the time.

Many factors influence our everyday lives. Our walk is always under construction. When we embrace that, our steps will be on the correct road! We banish fear when we know the entire truth! We learn to think outside the box. That opens us to unlimited possibilities. We don't have to fear the future, because we are being rooted in good soil. We don't stress over anything! We follow a map of Harmony! Our openness to the Spirit within supplies us with vitality and harmony. We can then become leaders for those who are still lost! People can't see, nor can they appreciate our positive qualities, if we're stuck under a pile of negativity!

Through prayer and effort, we can stop a negative pattern before it becomes a way of life. That's entirely different than the concept of "mind over matter". We cannot *think* our way to strength or victory. But we can speak strength and victory instead of sadness and fear! Our spoken words aren't simply sounds we make. They're the overflow of our hearts. They possess power. That which possesses the inner chambers of our hearts also dictates to what flows from our lips. Words don't just convey information; they can destroy someone's spirit. They can ignite hatred and violence. But, if our hearts are changed by the power of God, our words can also unleash miracles, so long as we utter them with faith.

Adopting a selfless attitude was a huge step for me. The more I wanted; the more I struggled. And when I coerced myself into an altruistic mentality; I struggled even more. I got mad at myself for not letting go of my own personal preferences. That was a problem for me because I was never allowed to have my own preferences growing up. I had to work hard to make it a new habit. It was hard to let it slip its moorings. I knew I had to let it happen because it was expected of me. This time, not as a defenseless little child; but as a person ready to fulfill heavenly expectations. So I started with giving away things that were of value to me; like a pretty frame I had set aside for myself, or a piece of costume jewelry someone admired on me, etc.   Giving to others is like saying farewell to something we will miss.   It's a lot different that offering something we no longer want. And it has nothing to do with exchanging goods like most of us do during Christmas.   Giving is more meaningful when we give to those who can't give back.

    I believe I went from one extreme to the other for a while.   I gave to liars!   I gave to cheats!   I gave to thieves!   And I gave to swine!   But I learned to give!   And gave without regrets!   If some of them were proud of themselves because they took advantage of my generosity; I was equally as proud; if not more.   Because I had given freely.   What they managed to take was actually given to them out of obedience to God.   How could I harbor anger towards people who didn't have a compassionate heart?   The kind of compassion that would make room for someone else's needs.   I don't believe any time soon; but maybe years later, their veil of misconception will be lifted, and they'll get to see my true character.   And who knows; God might even reveal to them all about this damaged little girl who simply wanted to be loved.   She wanted to convince the world she was worthy; and maybe she tried too hard!   I will never hear God say, "... my Good and faithful servant!   I'm well pleased with you; because you gave recklessly to those who didn't exalt my name for your efforts."   But I will hear Him say, "Good and faithful servant!   I'm well pleased with your obedience!"

    I didn't practice obedience to be right with God.   I did so, because I was already right with Him through my faith in His Son, Jesus the Christ.   I wanted to please Him because I was His child.   My desire to please Him came from an overflowing sense of gratitude. Nothing else! If I ever approach God with any hidden agenda, He know. I can be fooled very easily; because I'm a trusting person. I can even fool myself. But I can never fool Him. I read on a marquee once: "A hypocrite is a person who's not himself on Sunday." Jesus denounced the Pharisees because they spoke of their holiness; but their deeds didn't reflect the same. Jesus spoke harsh words against them; while He comforted the sinners.

For me to claim that I conquered life's obstacles all by myself would be foolish. I'm simply glad life didn't swallow me alive! Depression woke me up every morning. Self-doubt crept in every afternoon. Uncertainty summoned warnings and dangers. Panic stayed for dinner quite often. Insanity was just around the corner. But strength and good sense appeared just in time to help me make it through each day. Thinking small was my enemy during those years. Even baby steps were exhausting. But once I decided to have higher goals, then my obstacles seemed smaller. Because I was "fearfully and wonderfully made" by God. Every creation of His is a masterpiece. There is no reason to doubt it. I may feel down and depressed occasionally due to my limited thinking. But when I focus on the fact that God made me; then I am the way I'm supposed to be. I'm unique. I shouldn't strive to be like others. And with that notion in heart, I make a conscious effort to groom my character, instead of my ego.

Everyone walks through stages of self-doubt. We all have shifting and conflicting impulses. Spirit and matter aren't mutually exclusive. Though they are inseparable; they're separate life forms.

They are interdependent; yet they don't always complement one another. Our ultimate desire is to become whole. For me, the day my heart doesn't question my intellect is a good day. And when my intellect celebrates that which my heart is happy about, I'm at peace. That's how I want every day to be; effortless and serene.

  Each person's sense of purpose or fulfillment is different. For many, it's material at first. Climbing the corporate ladder could be one. Being fit and beautiful might be another. Recognition and appreciation are important to everyone. Accomplishments are rewarding. We pursue various goals, thinking they'll give us the satisfaction we're looking for. We chase after them for years; and sometimes, only to walk away empty handed. I stopped asking questions like "What is the meaning of life?" In my case, the answer is simple. I am the meaning of my life. It sounds selfish; but it's not. My purpose and my fulfillment are all about being the best that I can be. Nothing is external. I don't want to impress others. I just want to improve internally. More people see their obstacles as delays. I don't. My inopportune moments have been the keys to my spiritual promotions. They instilled fortitude in small measures I never had before. They squeezed the timid out of me; and gave me wings to soar to unknown altitudes. I'm happy to say my inner person and I are walking this journey together, until we are "one". And that is the true meaning of my life.

  Goals don't have to be long term. Even those that are short-term matter. I broke my left leg in two places during a bicycle accident. The condition I was in at the time is known as "a hairdresser's greatest nightmare". The paramedics arrived and took me straight to the emergency room. I received all kinds of attention; but no one discussed any details with me. I felt more broken. Frustration settled in. I kept my eyes fixed on the ceiling, in order to fight the tears. Forcing myself to be brave was overrated. I finally gave in and shifted my head toward the wall, and whispered, "Oh, how I need help!" Instantly I discerned a whisper from within saying, "You're not going to need surgery." My spirit was uplifted immediately. I was filled with hope. Only then did I notice someone in scrubs washing his hands, with his back to me. I sheepishly asked, "How much longer before someone sets my leg?" Without turning around to face me, he muttered, "Oh, we have prepped you for surgery. No one is setting your leg." I was puzzled and a bit angry. "I'm not having surgery. If you won't set my leg, then you'll have to release me", I said with an attitude. He finally turned around and explained: "I've consulted with two other surgeons. Your leg broke in a twisting position, leaving small particles here and there. There's no way this leg can be set successfully." I heard every word; but I had already heard greater words before this stranger spoke his. Within thirty minutes, upon my request, I was discharged with a prescription slip in my hand.

We stopped by the nearest pharmacy and had the prescription filled. As I finally laid on my own bed with my foot facing the back side of me, I felt at peace. I had followed my inner voice instead of being defeated by fear. I knew I was only at the beginning of my new journey. There was much to conquer. But God doesn't start us on a path if He's not going to help us make it all the way. As the pain killers calmed my nerves, I felt as though my entire body was being immersed into a sea of tranquility.

I gave in to their effects, and dove in.

    I woke up from a deep sleep the next morning with a name ringing in my ears, "Schreiber ...Schreiber ...Schreiber ..."   I asked to see the phone book; for I knew no one with that name.   But I somehow knew it had to be a physician.   And sure enough; there was an orthopedic surgeon with the name Dr. Schreiber.   I made an appointment to see him later that day.   When we arrived at his examining room, he told me he had already seen my x-rays; and there was no way that my leg could be set.   The missing little bone particles made it impossible to accomplish a good result without a surgery.   Again, I was hearing him; but I had already believed my inner voice.   So I begged, "If you would be so kind to give my body a chance to heal, I know it will.   Pretty please..."   After several versions of the same plea, he finally gave in, and agreed to set my leg.   He took another x-ray to make sure both my Tibia and Fibula were properly lined up, somewhat in the proper position.   He wanted me to come back in two weeks so he could x-ray my leg again.   If they hadn't shifted from their present position, then we did have a winner.   His instructions were for me to stay in bed with my leg elevated until then.

    That didn't happen.   I was at work the next morning, cutting hair, seated in a wheel chair.   We had replaced my big hydraulic chair with a little stool so I could be slightly taller than my customers.   The taller customers had to scoot down so I could perform better.   But everyone supported me.   In two weeks, I received a great report from the surgeon; and the rest is history.   I stayed in a full cast for about six weeks; and was upgraded to a smaller one afterward.   Some people commented I was going to feel that pain for the rest of my life.   I looked them straight in the eyes and said, "God's healing comes without conditions. He's never said He would heal me this once; but I'm on my own when it rains". They stared at me as if I had three heads. I either believe in God or I don't. Believing in Him has no grey areas. His unconditional love is hundred percent through our innocence. It's there at birth all the way to the end; if we'll have it.

    I believe newborns' innocence is anything but emptiness. Instead, it holds treasures unknown to man; because that new person is already equipped with heavenly resources. They don't just disappear because they never had a chance to materialize. Instead, they remain hidden; and every now and then, they torment us. Just because babies can't physically care for themselves, it doesn't mean they are blank canvases. They are fully capable of following their own dreams; because they possess all the necessary tools. We, as parents, look after them, love and guard them against all obstacles; until they're awakened to the pursuit of their own happiness. They don't all just wake up to the right idea one morning. Some arrive there through the process of elimination. Or it's an ongoing operation of hit-or-miss for others. Our position in their lives is to identify and observe their traits and aptitudes. We may gently correct them; and always encourage and enable them to find the path to their own future. If we don't believe in our children; how are we to teach them to believe in themselves? And how could we entertain such a thought, if we don't believe in God who preps them for their own life journey; way before we get to hold them in our arms? Babies seem helpless at the beginning; but are they really? Through their innocence, they stay connected to their Maker; who is the supreme parent of all past, present, and future.

I don't agree with those who claim babies are born in sin. Scripture teaches us that, at death, "the dust will return to the earth as it was, and the spirit will return to God who gave it."   The parents do not give the spirit to a child.   God does.   Since God rejects sin and creates life, He is the giver of the spirit.   I believe a newborn baby's soul cannot be sinful.   Verses like "in sin my mother conceived me" might lead us to certain misinterpretations.   Let's just say, if our father whips us in his drunkenness, should we attribute drunkenness to ourselves?   That doesn't make sense.   The following verse clarifies some of that confusion: "The person who sins will die.   The son will not bear the punishment for the father's iniquity."   Any misconception we have is detailed and explained in the Bible.   We need to read it with a willingness to comprehend; so the Holy Spirit can bring us to a heavenly understanding.   Those explanations are not transmitted through outward channels.   They're inward revelations; inside each person, under piles of the do's and the don'ts of the world, along with personal hurts and disappointments.   These are the building blocks of each individual, and they are the guaranteed aspects of life; since most people choose individuality over unity.

The one who was the most surprised over the healing of my leg without a surgery was my mother.   She said to me one day, "I still don't know how you pulled that off!"   Acting as if I didn't know what she was referring to, I asked, "Pulled what off?"   She replied, "Hobbling around and cutting hair with a broken leg."   The answer was simple, "Mom, I never thought for a second that the things I get to accomplish everyday were my own doing.   So I simply believed when there was less of me; there would be more of Him.   That's all.   And I was solid in that belief.   I didn't give fear a chance to penetrate and steal the perfect result from me." I suspect she didn't quite get it; but that's all I could do. I shared my testimony and left it at that. People who have ears to hear, will hear; without my perseverance. Evil teaches us hurt and deceit. But we can overcome evil by repeating: We belong to the invincible God.

I once listened to my pastor preach about "hurt people, hurt people". I didn't make the connection then; but I now understand why. Hurt people often transfer their anger onto their family and close friends. Because of their pain, ordinary words are interpreted as something negative toward them. Because they've been victimized in their lives, they carry a "victim" spirit. Rage is their only language. Though they alienate others; in the end they wonder why no one is there for them. Often they have the emotional maturity of the age when they received their now buried hurt. I was about forty-two when I remembered something awful from the past. The pain came back to me as if I were that seven-year-old little girl. That shows me there might be many more that I'm not aware of yet. And by the same token, I don't know how deep my mother's pain is buried. I can only hope and pray that she won't remember. As mean as she was to me; I still don't want her to hurt over things she can do nothing about.

It's possible to feel sorry for those who have offended us. Though we are their temporary victim; they seem to be trapped in their confused state of mind for life. It's a cycle most of them can't get out of. I remember how quiet my parents' home was toward the end. Dad, afraid of verbal attacks, agreed with Mom almost all the time; and answered when asked. He had his writings that honed his communication skills. But Mom was alone in the deafening silence she had created.   She had no one to talk to.   She became the victim of her own doing.   I had also cautioned myself against her.   I would be on the phone with Dad, laughing and carrying on; when suddenly she would take the receiver away from him and ask, "What are you two laughing about?"   I immediately sunk into my selective mutism, knowing I needed to weigh and measure every word from then on.   Again Mom's result was a hush.   To this day, she still doesn't know why she never heard the stories and the laughter Dad and I shared.   I feel sad for her; because she missed so much.   We weren't alienating her; we were trying to dodge her insulting darts.   If only she would stop being so controlling, and enjoy life's tender moments with us!   But it wasn't meant to be.

    Until every soul is free to investigate its past, it is stuck in the cycles of believing we're here to suffer the consequences of living in a cruel world.   Our approach to those delicate issues needs to be proactive; if we want to be liberated from the tyranny of their hold.   Otherwise we'll remain enslaved until the end; not knowing which direction to face.   If we're willing to look past them, and write them off as opportunities for growth, we've got miracles to unleash and live through.   Not only do they shape and mold us into a better and wiser person; they also teach us how to adapt to changes.   And if we refrain from blaming the other person; we better understand our own contribution to the matter at hand.   A positive approach will help remember each lesson when a similar challenge confronts us.   In fact, a whole new reality emerges from it.

    This may sound peculiar but, sooner or later, our past comes to our rescue.   We cannot deny that truth.   That's why we should never wish to forget it.   It has a tremendous amount of guidance and power to help us through future challenges.   The mine fields we walked through once upon a time are now the stepping stones of fortitude and resilience.   As we strive toward the shining pinnacle of refinement; complaining about the past loses its importance.   After all, negativity can never birth anything of value.   It makes us lethargic and barren.   Although, there are people who are addicted to negativity.   Ironically, they seek out experiences and situations that stimulate negative feelings.   They're rarely happy.   And if a good solution erases what they've been fussing over; they'll come up with something new to complain about in no time.   Negativity is like a drug to them.   By fueling their anger and bitterness, it validates their unhappy identity.   Pity or sympathy for them is like receiving a standing ovation from their audience.   Even though they get on our nerves; they're to be pitied.

    Our mental pinnacle is achieved by transitioning our past into our future, from a positive perspective.   If we claim to be limping because someone injured us years ago; that's what we'll be doing for the rest of our lives.   But if we believe we can be restored to health, regardless of the damages; we can.   If our bodies are designed to heal themselves while we rest or sleep; how much more should we expect from our spiritual bodies; knowing our spirit source is God.   Getting adequate rest improves our physical and mental health; while adding quality to our lives.   Prayer has the same effect on our spiritual body. It actually begins with God's call to us; not the other way around. "Come to me, all you who are weary and burdened", He says.   We don't always hear His invitation; because we are too busy handling everything.   Yet when we listen and respond to His call, we take time out from all exertion.   Our lives will be a paradise when we set aside all management and manipulation; in order to recover our strength and forbearance to enjoy our fullest life.

What determines how far is far enough depends on each person's ability to look Fear in the Face, and say, "You are toast; because I belong!" When we realize the power within that sentence, then the sky is the limit. We can look at past damages and smirk with disdain. When we assume the full responsibility and attitude of a conqueror - and we are more than conquerors - we don't learn from our past; the past learns from us. People who took advantage of their position in my life aren't happy with my progress. How can a mother be happy with herself for decimating her own child's self-worth and emotional development? What kind of threat could a little girl pose to a parent that a battle against her innocence becomes necessary? And those who tried to destroy her remnants also had nothing to teach. If anything, they learned something valuable from me: "You cannot bully those who belong to God; lest you better be prepared to face Him."

This is my story and I'm proud to tell it! All of my challenges so far helped me build a bridge between the past and the future. I have stopped questioning wickedness because it'll never make sense. It's a lost cause. I cherish my new attitude. It's a decision. I wasn't born with it. It gave me a fresh start. Yet this particular one doesn't involve something new. It just involves letting go of something old. This precious life is a gift. It is worth every effort in order to savor each moment as if it is our last. And I truly believe we can all grow to be a child; set aside our fears; put on a smile; close our eyes; and dance like nobody's watching!

ACKNOWLEDGEMENTS

My sincerest gratitude to God for keeping me devoid of unnecessary anger and bitterness toward those I was commanded to love; and for honing the gift of patience in the interim. I am thankful that my father, Berc Cerrahyan, taught me what a true hero is all about without displaying conspicuous acts of bravery; but by simply serving those under his care. Life wouldn't be worth living without my brother Jirayr, and my children Iris and Osheen.

And I also want to recognize all of my friends for standing by me and encouraging me through thick and thin; especially Kathleen McBlair, Sheila Kilpatrick, and Irwin Wells, for taking the time to examine my pages with scrupulous attention to detail. Success is a byproduct of unity with which I am blessed.

Made in the USA
Middletown, DE
27 February 2017